UNCONSCIOUS

UNCONSCIOUS

UNLOCKING THE ZONE OF EXTRAORDINARY PERFORMANCE

J. W. Walker

euthus
PUBLISHING

ISBN: 9798695419016

FIRST EDITION

Scripture taken from King James Version and
the Literal Translation of the Holy Bible
Copyright © 1976 - 2000
By Jay P. Green, Sr.
Used by permission of the copyright holder.

Cover design *"Neural Networks"* by J. W. Walker

This publication is designed to provide accurate information regarding the subject matter covered. It is offered and should be read with the understanding that the author and publisher are not engaged in rendering medical or psychological service. This book is not intended to be a substitute for therapy or professional advice.

Euthus Publishing
Houston, TX

CONTENTS

To Mom and in memory of Dad.

Introduction

"Man is a wonderful, inconceivably complex being.
Consider the facts:..."
—Werner Gitt

This book is about us—it's about you and me; It's about our potential; It's about *incidents* of incredible human performance, often seen in athletes, geniuses, sudden super heroes, and others.

If we didn't have proof of its existence, we might think this idea of a "**zone** of super human performance" is the product of fantasy and imagination; but our venture is only in the world of reality.

What do Hurricane Sandy, the woman who lifted the car off her dad, Typhoon Haiyan (the greatest storm to ever strike land), the man who became a genius after a brutal mugging, J. K. Rowling, and Tiger Woods, have in common?

Think about the hurricane, tornado, earthquake—all of these natural phenomena. What do they say to us? They occur, and make their mark in a powerful and convincing way. We hurry to forget, clear our minds, and hope they will not return; but we can't ignore their power when they arise and disrupt our normality. They are all forces to be *reckoned* with.

So it is with the **incidents** of The Zone Phenomenon (TZP). Are we supposed to act like it doesn't mean anything? We may minimize or ignore its influence, and forget its brief appearances, but it too is undeniably a considerable force. It shakes our perception and reality.

Consider this book the reckoning with this phenomenon.

Welcome to UNCONSCIOUS: Secrets of The Zone Phenomenon, learned and deciphered from those who have personally experienced its power, and recorded here, for those who want to experience it.

At first glance the comparison between natural, often catastrophic phenomena, and exceptionally performing human beings, seems to be out of place, and a stretch of the imagination—but, as you will see, the connection is warranted. The psychological and philosophical impact of these phenomena should be nothing less than profound to us.

The impact on our world, and the message these phenomena send, is like seeing meteorites hit the earth again and again but acting as if it doesn't mean anything.

I believe we have in fact ignored, or at least misinterpreted, the significance of these incidents of super human performance we've witnessed quite frequently in our world. These episodes beg to be understood for what they mean for human potential.

Perhaps The Zone asserts its power and influence to tell us something about ourselves that we are unaware of, or carelessly overlook. The tornado tells us how comparatively small and powerless we can be. **But, maybe the Zone Phenomenon tells us how powerful we could be—our true potential?**

I'm convinced answers should be sought, not only in the slow probing of science, but also in the areas of religion and philosophy—after all we are dealing with *super* natural things. There is enough substance in these occurrences of extraordinary human performance witnessed in sports, music, arts, and ordinary life, to draw some definite conclusions about the nature of these powerful events, and their meaning to each of us.

As to the question "what about me, the average Joe?" "Can I access this potential?" "Are you saying I can unlock the gate into my latent, super potential?" Well, let me say: there are clear identifiable paths toward it, keys to unlock the gate, and laws which govern this distinct region of transcendent human performance. This is my conclusion after years of observation, investigation, and research. That important "me" question is answered a number of ways throughout this book.

This book proceeds from the principle: We can't utilize what we have no knowledge or understanding of. Also, what we don't know can sometimes hurt us, and will likely hinder us.

Therefore, questions regarding the nature of the phenomenon—**what** it is, **how** it functions, and what **causes** it to happen—are answered first. How, and which parts of the human body are involved in producing the experience, and the extraordinary performance, are answered?

I hope to prove that we are indeed more than we dare to imagine. Every one of us is phenomenal, and most of us have untapped potential! The super powerful microscopes through which scientists examine our smallest parts prove it. Did you know that the sacred letter to the Hebrews states that angels in heaven are appointed to serve mankind—does the greater serve the lesser? We are something special. But, I'm getting ahead of myself.

Because we are all unique, reaching our true individual potential may very well look different for each one of us. Although we are made the same, the final product (the way in which our body, brain, and mind, express themselves), is different for each of us. To reach this **latent** potential, the previously mentioned knowledge and understanding are essential.

Later in the book the external factors and circumstances which contribute to, and cause the phenomenon, will be discussed; all in an effort to hopefully reproduce the results in our own lives. Next, after understanding how it happens, the contributions our bodies make, and the special circumstances involved, we will consider some of the negative things we do which prevent us from performing at our maximum potential. The often misunderstood component of "peak" human performance is: identifying and avoiding the barriers which would prevent optimal performance. If you are hindered your performance **cannot** reach its potential.

We are in an age and culture that places little value on preventing ills, but rather, relies on some "secret pill" or operation to correct (mostly counteract) the negative consequences of careless living and decision making. In my opinion, this kind of mentality lacks understanding, and contributes to all kinds of human malfunction and dysfunction which plague our species—including mediocre performance. So, expect no magic key to unlock the gate into extraordinary performance which doesn't also include understanding and *care*-fullness.

This point will become clearer in the section on *Road-blocks, Pitfalls, Obstacles, and Barriers*. In other words, we will take an objective and a subjective look at the phenomenon,, with the goal of deriving as much personal benefit as possible. I believe "knowledge is **potential** power". Understanding and wisdom, (true knowledge *applied* and *lived*) is real power.

Although I use creative writing and imagery as much as possible in this book, it is only because this subject invites it, and captivates the imagination. I do my best to avoid turning things which pertain to our real world and life into mere fantasy and fiction. This book is non-fiction, and hopefully contributes to the understanding of ourselves, and the improvement of our condition.

One of my favorite sections of the book derives some meaning from this phenomenon: answering the questions "what does this mean", and "are we more then we dare to imagine?"

I began my investigation simply to understand how "The Zone" phenomenon worked in sports, and whether or not its power was available to everyone. The deeper I traveled into this **territory**, the wider its influence, and the more the notions of "freak occurrence" and "accidental genius" fell by the wayside, and the reality of some kind of inherent, latent potential became obvious.

The book UNCONSCIOUS is certainly a healthy snack for those who are super naturally inclined. Quite a few of the books written on the subject of extraordinary human performance have concluded some involvement of supernatural forces. I recently read a review on a book about child prodigies, criticizing the author for suggesting "re-incarnation" as a possible cause of a five year old child's incredible music ability. Although I personally reject the idea of re-incarnation, I too am convinced *supernatural human ability* deserves to be considered as the result of some kind of *supernatural influence*. Until these types of occurrences become normal everyday experiences, they demand our minds venture beyond the common place.

I must re-iterate, I have an aversion to fiction—my mind just doesn't work that way. I prefer to spend my limited time exploring, reading, and learning facts. So, for entertainment I can *tolerate* fiction that is based on truth. However, I purpose to ground any of my "supernatural" conclusions in this non-fiction book on tangible facts.

It will be necessary for you to read the entire book so that you can appreciate the conclusions drawn toward the end... whether you embrace them or not.

I welcome any discussion via my blog un-conscious.com or e-mail joe@un-conscious.com.

I hope you enjoy reading this book as much as I enjoyed writing it. Without further delay let our journey begin.

CHAPTER ONE

The Phenomenon

"All gather to see, what excitement there will be. A record to break, a spectacular feat, a performer transcend the bounds of man"
—jw

Remember the old television show—still on cable—*The Twilight Zone*, which was very popular years ago? When I began to write this book, seeking to quantify this phenomenon, the origins of the phrase "The Zone," and its mystical type of experience: that old TV show and its introduction came to mind. I literally smiled with fond memories of the mood set by the narrated introduction. I am doubtful that show is the source of the use of the phrase in sports, but that is all I could come up with as to origins.

I am pleased to say, there are indeed similarities between the show's poetic intro to that make-believe "twilight zone" and the real life "zone phenomenon" experience. Allow me to draw some comparison between the two—assuming good fiction has a basis in reality. (Rod Sterling's intro was such good creative writing and narration.) Here is a line from one of several brilliant intros:

"You're traveling through another dimension—a dimension not only of sight and sound, but of mind..."

- The Zone Phenomenon (TZP) is similarly another dimension, in the sense that ordinary time and space are experienced in a different way. There is no actual new dimension, just an enhanced experience of the dimension of space and time in which we live.

- The Zone is a dimension of mind, and I would add senses, depending on the demands and requirements of the task being performed. The demands of the athlete, artist, scientist, or musician for example are all different in The Zone. More on this later.

- The Zone is definitely a journey into a state of super performance, which for many is pleasant and desirable, but regrettably—for most—short lived.

- The TV show was an adventure in a mental world of make-believe, the dimension was fantasy—like the world of dreams. The real Zone Phenomenon is not make-believe at all; rather, it is literal reality,, on a level we don't get a chance to see very often. Let's say it is a window into true potential, not fantasy but real, tangible potential.

This comparison simply scratches the surface of what TZP is. I would encourage you—for entertainment—to check out the brief bio on Rod Sterling and the show online; his talent and work are very fascinating.

The mysterious aspects of the real Zone Phenomenon can't be ignored.

MY JOURNEY BEGAN

Sometime around 1994, while exhibiting at a sports trade show, I met a former Major League Baseball player named Lem P. Our conversation turned toward his experiences of being "in The Zone" and what it felt like. I recall what he said because it was so interesting that I began to convert the concepts to poetry.

My memory and notes remind me that he shared experiencing the sensation of a trance like state (which I can only understand by associating it with hypnosis), in which the stitches of the baseball, approaching at 90 plus miles per hour, could be counted...all noise is muffled, and solid contact between bat and ball is certain.

At that time, I began to experiment with graphic ideas for T-shirts that would capture the experience Lem described, along with ideas I developed from observing athletes who appeared to be performing in The Zone, particularly basketball great, Michael Jordan.

Since that time I have taken up the game of golf, and have experienced one occasion of being in The Zone. This was several years ago when my average score was around 95. Much to the astonishment of my playing partners—one, a very good long time friend, who is was is at least 15 strokes better than me—I was playing in The Zone. I was swinging the club and hitting the ball like I had been playing my whole life. I was unflappable. It was easy. I hit the ball where I wanted, and ended up shooting 15 strokes better than my average, (I scored 80), equaling my good friend, who has played his whole life.

Needless to say, I have been looking for The Zone—on that level—ever since. My scores are much better now, around 84 on average, thanks to experience and practice. (We can per-form well at almost anything we apply ourselves to, but "The Zone" is a higher level of performance.)

If you are a serious athlete or sports fan, you have no doubt experienced or witnessed "The Zone". You may be involved in performance other than sports, and like me, be longing to witness or experience it again.

There are many books and theories circulating about what I am referring to as The Zone Phenomenon. They may ap-proach this phenomenon from the perspective of a "higher level of consciousness," a "super conscious mind," or some other idea, in an attempt to explain this experience, and teach us how to tap into this power. I'm not attempting to do that, because I am persuaded this phenomenon is essentially an "unconscious" state.

What we know for sure, from history and experience, is that no one has been successful at teaching anyone how to "tap into" this zone-like state through a deliberate act of the will or training. If they could, we would have—by this time in history—a super group of extraordinary human beings, or maybe even a nation of them, operating on a continual high level of proficiency, creativity, and accomplishment that we only see in brief spurts when we witness or experience The Zone. That "you can tap-in" philosophy, in my opinion, en-courage feelings of inadequacy in those who can't "tap in", and a false sense of superiority in those who convince themselves they have. As we will see later, although our brains have the same parts, each individual uses his brain in different ways, so no single formula would work for everyone.

But, I will tell you, in the same way a parent or teacher

may recognize exceptional talent in a child, and encourage its development; those who are somehow suited to perform in The Zone, are likely to experience it more often than others. (I am hinting at "talent" here, a subject we'll talk about later.) This is a fact that is proven by history and observation. Many of our public and private primary school systems are correct to recognize youth who fit the "gifted and talented" programs. You may very well be one of those individuals.

I don't personally believe these facts relegate the rest of us to the sidelines to only observe this phenomenon in others. As I mentioned earlier, I have experienced it myself and I am by no means a gifted athlete. Albeit my experience was not the world record-breaking zone experience of Annika Sorenstam, which I'll share in the next chapter.

Our Expedition Plan

To give you a better understanding of what The Zone is, I want us to first get a picture of the region through its inhabitants. Then we'll explore the rest of this incredible territory, including the *high performance* territory just outside its walls. You see, there appears to be a well populated region of performance just below *transcendent*.

A very good way to learn about any country or region of this world is to get to know its people. Unfortunately, this is the only way for many of us who haven't experienced it to know what The Zone is like.

Understanding this phenomenon is a matter of interpretation, as this subject is shrouded with mystery. Although it is frequent enough for us to be familiar with some aspects of the subject, it is elusive enough to prevent a clear understanding of its dynamics. Almost every author on the subject of super human performance will draw different conclusions about the questions of how and why. (Although, many books add little new information, they just repackage old information.)

It will however become evident that *no one* just *decides* to go into The Zone at will. (I am not convinced by the claims of eastern mystics and their meditation.) This state is accessible by invitation only. This includes the super gifted such as prodigies and geniuses. This fact supports and strengthens my conclusion that it is indeed an involuntary or "unconscious" state. Its unconscious nature also adds to its mystery. So then, because it is a desirable destination, it is considered *beneficium* (a privilege) to receive an invitation—or better yet—to be ***drafted*** into its domain.

If you haven't *yet* received an invitation, you will have to —in the meantime—rely mostly on the testimony of others, and your own observation from a distance.

Perhaps, if you know where and when this phenomenon is likely to strike—like a tornado chaser—you can put yourself in its path.

CHAPTER TWO

The Inhabitants

*"The so-called Zone is a temporary place of residence.
Sorry, no baggage allowed, so leave the text book at home.
It's a district with its own rules and boundaries—NONE!"*

—jw

A lec Kornacki lies in a bed in Virginia Commonwealth University Medical Center with five fractured ribs, a fractured sternum and vertebrae, and some damage to his right arm. He's a fortunate guy. You see, had not his daughter been there for him, he would have certainly died. She was granted temporary access to The Zone.

July 29, 2012 Mr. Kornacki was working under his car when it collapsed on top of him, pinning his right arm on top of his chest, rendering him unconscious, and not breathing. His 22 year old daughter, Lauren, found him pinned; and without thinking, lifted the car which weighed about a ton and a half, moved it over, pulled her dad free, and administered CPR until he regained consciousness. This event—like many Zone *incidents*—made national news headlines.

A couple of weeks later in Brockton Massachusetts, a man named Carlos Castro lifted an SUV to save his friend.[1]

~

As far as I can determine the residents of The Zone can be divided into two categories: temporary and permanent. The difference is the amount of time a person remains within this powerful region before he is expelled.

When I first became aware of this state of transcendent human performance, I associated it exclusively with the temporary residents I observed or who had returned from The Zone to share their experiences.

Most of you have also witnessed the power of The Zone while a temporary resident like the automobile lifters, an athlete or musician—was for a time—operating under the power of its influence. However, it was particularly intriguing for me to discover the existence of permanent residents: people like "super heroes" living constantly within the boundaries of The Zone's powerful influence.

Let's examine the temporary residents first, and the power source before we visit the permanent residents.

TEMPORARY RESIDENTS

Aliens and Transients

Author J. K. Rowling, in a recent interview, discussed her extended but temporary visit to The Zone, where she conceived and wrote the Harry Potter series. She sincerely believes that

---

[1] http://un-conscious.com/videos/man-lifts-suv-saves-his-friend/

this "once in a lifetime," transcendent, inspirational experience will never be repeated in her life. *"Lightning never strikes the same place twice,"* she reasoned. Her statement acknowledges the *transient* and *privileged* nature of The Zone Phenomenon.

It appears, after sharing a place atop the pinnacle of creative success, she sees herself once again on the outside of The Zone region. Welcome back! Who knows, an invitation may unexpectedly arrive again someday.

I find this noteworthy: if Mrs. Rowling had contributed her incredibly successful *Potter* creation to talent, for instance, she could expect to repeat it; but she obviously considers that stroke of genius: *transcendent*, above her natural or acquired ability. Therefore, it is similar to a unexpected yet fortuitous "strike of lightning." I call this a *temporary* Zone residence—a short term invitation to extraordinary human performance.

∽

It was early 2010, I'm watching a professional golf tournament on TV. All the talk was about Nick Watney, a player who was eight under par on the front nine holes, threatening to set a new Professional Golf Association tournament record.

For those unfamiliar with golf: A round (game) of golf is played on 18 separate 'holes,' each set-up to take a certain number of "strokes" (strikes) of the golf ball to put that little white ball into the distant hole with the flag sticking out. The task is made difficult by strategically placed obstacles and hazards, like water, trees, sand bunkers, and deep grass. Each of the 18 holes is designed to play in three, four, or five strokes (the number which determines "par" for that hole). One stroke under par is called a "birdie." Nick Watney made eight birdies out of nine holes, including two holes which he played in only two strokes.

He was in "The Zone." That kind of performance is also referred to as "unconscious," as both words describe the trance-like state. Nick was unconscious on the first nine holes, but then he "woke up" on the last nine holes to shoot—a mere mortal—one stroke under par. Mr. Watney finished with a very impressive total score of nine under par.

Whenever an athlete (or other performer) performs in an exceptional way while at the same time his fellow competitors, under the same conditions, are being taught a lesson by the game, it's a good bet that player is in The Zone. He or she has performed to near perfection under conditions which, by all reasonable expectations, would not allow such a performance. When this happens on a professional level, it is all the more incredible because of the level of difficulty, talent and expertise. At this level the game is *designed* to be tougher, and the competitors are equally talented and experienced—they're the best. Therefore, when a single player transcends the game and his peers, it is recognized for the outstanding and remarkable feat it is. If it is record breaking—such as Jim Furyk's incredible 59 round—it has the additional benefit of raising the bar of expectations for human potential in that sport, and the hearts of everyone who witnessed it.

This *potential for* transcendent performance, I found to be a key contributor to the passion and fanaticism which fuels the love for sports all over the world. The very same expectations are a part of all artistic performances. In my opinion this expectation is well deserved. I personally believe we are capable of more, and I enjoy seeing my expectations confirmed.

⌇

I remember watching Michael Jordan around the time I became acquainted and fascinated with the idea of the *so-called* Zone. I now believe it is rightly called "The Zone" as opposed to "a zone;". That is, there is but one region or state wherein this phenomenon is experienced. Although the circumstances and manifestations (gifts) are different, the source is the same.

Back to Jordan: I was fascinated by Michael Jordan because he appeared to play in The Zone more than other top athletes. When you are talking about an athlete standing out among the greatest players in the world, it is obvious you are witnessing something special. The Zone at that level is near the pinnacle of human potential in athletic performance. The Zone *forces* its subject (like a complicit captive) to play above his normal abilities, it commandeers all resources.

I must interject at this point: I don't believe in the worship of any human being (except Jesus Christ). The involuntary aspect of TZP make it clear that the subject of its power may have some contribution to the experience, but that contribution is minimal, considering the level of perfection produced. The subject's own account also confirm he/she was under some greater, outside influence. So, not to undermine the hero— just careful not to bestow credit where it doesn't belong.

When Jordan would drive into the well-guarded painted area of the court, (everyone expected him to go to the hoop for an easy lay-up or dunk), all of the defense would collapse on him. He would appear to hang in mid-air until everyone else came down, or a crack of daylight revealed itself. Then he would gracefully maneuver through the available space between defenders, and put the ball into the basket. He did this time and time again.

There is no doubt that advertising and marketing helped to make Jordan the world phenomenon he became, but he still had to live up to the hype, and set those records.

This is another excellent example of the reality and powers of TZP. Some players make it look so easy that if we are not careful, we will take it for granted. Many of the other accomplished players Jordan played with and against were happy—in the face of opposition—to draw a foul and head for the free-throw line; Jordan regularly finished the play by scoring the basket—undaunted by the obstacles in front of him. Therein, we find another key to greatness, which we will examine later in the book.

It is easy for us to get caught up in the emotions of watching great performances, and neglect to consider the deeper meaning of that to which we are witnesses. **When we contemplate the split second decisions, agility, control, and opposing forces at work, it is easier to appreciate what is happening here, and the difficult task accomplished.** These factors are present in all athletic competition. Unfortunately, we are prone to under-appreciate the complexity until something like age related deterioration or injury make it not so easy to perform—then we enjoy the memories.

You may even remember the ads run by Jordan's shoe company giving credit to the shoes for such feats. You may also recall those ads helped them sell warehouses full of shoes. But I am here to tell you, it wasn't "the shoes." It was either exceptional talent (we will discuss talent later), and/or the influence of The Zone.

◇

Another example, revealing another aspect of The Zone phenomenon, was Muhammad Ali's victory over George Foreman at the *"Rumble in the Jungle."* Very few experts believed Ali could beat Foreman toe to toe, that included Ali himself, who developed the (famous and shockingly passive) *"rope-a-dope"* strategy, to win the fight. I include this historic feat in TZP, because it was transcendent and improbable; Ali had to tap into resources beyond what he typically used. Also, he had to accurately calculate and predict his opponent's actions, in order to enable survival, and ultimate victory. That feat highlights an aspect of The Zone that is often overlooked or underrated: *"a need to succeed"*—(A Key? I'll elaborate later.) **The Zone takes potential, and multiplies it.**

◇

Annika Sorenstam dominated women's golf, winning 90 international tournaments as a professional. She described the day she shot the lowest score on record for a professional female golfer, as feeling easy, (a common *feeling* in The Zone). She birdied eight of the first nine holes (like Nick Watney), and four on the back nine. *"The hole looked like a big bucket,"* she said. Annika said, it was so easy she didn't understand why she couldn't do it again.

Another interesting comment she made about that record setting day, was that a score of 54 (golf perfection!) was something—years earlier—she and her junior golf friends had talked about as a very real possibility. *(Another Zone Key?)*

When asked how close she has come to *The Zone* on other occasions, she said, *"Players work hard to find a balance, har-*

mony, and concentration that will result in The Zone." I detected a note of disappointment in her tone, having not found the key to return to the illusive Zone during a stellar career.

Annika has raised the bar for what is possible in golf for all who play, and will play in the future. This is an important story as we consider the possibilities of human achievement, our expectations, and the demands placed on the top athletes who fuel our passion for the games. It is their contributions to the game that should matter, not unreal expectations of unending super performance. More on this later.

∾

Speaking of contribution, possibilities, expectations, and The Zone, let's look at Tiger Woods. (I hope to draw more conclusions from each of these examples of "TZP" in the following chapters of the book.)

I guess we fans can thank God that every decade or so our expectations of transcending the bounds of human achievement are realized through some new "Phenom".

If you think about the long history of golf as a sport, the great players who came before Tiger, and what he has done to raise the bar of possibility, it's no wonder he is the most popular athlete in the world. We love our sports heroes because we love our sports.

I am not going to attempt to list his credits, but I will say, as relates to our topic, he appeared to own a permanent residence in The Zone for about 10 years after he became a professional. I will discuss a theory, as to why he received his Zone invitation, later in the book.

He has elevated what we believe is possible in the game of golf. Many current players, teachers, and fans have changed the way they approach the game because of his accomplishments. Not to mention what the game expects from him because of his past performance. It is literally incredible. For that reason I would be remiss (and an alien from another planet) to overlook him in this discussion.

Maybe studying him can help us answer the question that we all want to know...**can you access The Zone at will?** Can someone own a key? Also, how much does talent contribute to an athlete's ability to play in The Zone? What about gifts: is there such a thing?

The Moral Question

Before we go further, let me answer a question or objection some of my readers will have. How can I ignore Tiger's scandalous transgressions, and recommend him as an example? Frankly, if people of *apparent* excellent moral character were the only ones worthy to be considered in the search for human potential, this book would be very thin, because I haven't met a person with flawless character; A friend recently reminded me of the great Babe Ruth's—baseball Zone Resident—scandalous reputation.

Experience has taught me, that you will need to live with the person you *believe* to be perfect, to discover (along with that person's close family), that he or she doesn't come close to perfection. This is the sad, but true human condition.

I am interested in the maximum potential of human beings as a species—period! It doesn't matter to me in whom that potential manifests itself. Wherever it appears I will investigate. Therefore, many of the people I examine in this book, (whose lives are public) had/have great weaknesses—

moral and otherwise. Remember this "privilege" is "involuntary"...these people are "recipients" not "originators" of this phenomenon. *As a matter of fact, the more flawed the vessel, the greater the wonder of the phenomenon.*

However, this does raise a host of questions as to why, and how this phenomenon operates as it does—questions I will tackle in later chapters.

I get excited every time I behold TZP with my eyes, or hear a news report confirming its presence. You will also before you finish this book.

Musical Inspiration

In an interview aired on April 15, 2011, Motown great, Smokey Robinson, spoke of an occasion during which he sat at the piano with "Marvin," while he was writing the classic album *What's Going On.* Marvin Gaye told him he was not writing this album, "God was!" By the way, Smokey, an accomplished song writer himself, intimately familiar with human potential in song writing, music composition and performance said: "*When you listen to it (the album), I believe him.*"

What an acknowledgement from an artist who believed he was performing beyond his considerable, natural ability. My first reaction was to assume a Zone-like experience, where the music and lyrics flowed with little (if any) deliberate effort from his conscience mind. Or, every difficulty relating to the composition was quickly solved with the perfect answer. This is, of course, an assumption on my part, but if one believes "God" is doing something, it certainly can't be hard. Marvin Gaye, no doubt, experienced the sensation of being carried away to a zone far beyond his normal ability.

I was delighted to find the following quote on a website chronicling that epic album:

"The production of What's Going On is a remarkable mix of Motown talent and musicianship gained over decades of practice and performance... For 10 days in March 1971, Gaye and his team were in a zone of brilliance"[2]

This is not a unique experience among great musicians and composers. Arthur M. Abell in his book *Talks with Great Composers,* shares very similar expressions of involuntary inspiration from the likes of Beethoven, Strauss, and Brahms. Some of whom expressed a prophetic type of inspiration, which we associate with the likes of Moses and other Biblical writers.

Although interesting and compelling, I would hesitate to accept anything less than *absolute* perfection as directly "inspired by God"—in the Biblical sense. I believe we humans have demonstrated enough latent potential in our brains to be responsible for the magnificent feats of genius we have witnessed in these great musicians. In other words, TZP is so powerful and transcendent, that the experience may be contributed directly to God, in an attempt to pinpoint an immediate cause. (I have no problem with God as the ultimate cause, but directly, as in biblical inspiration, I hesitate). Nonetheless, their performances were often transcendent—super-natural to observers, and apparently overwhelming to themselves. We venture on for answers...

---

[2] http://whatsgoingonnow.org/music/studio-ten-days-snake-pit

Two Competitors in The Zone

What happens when two competitors are observed in The Zone at the same time? You may have heard the old baseball "great pitcher vs. great hitter debate;" or Superman vs. Batman superhero debate. Well, I believe this is exactly what happened on June 22, 2010 when John Isner of the United States, met Nicolas Mahut of France, for their fifth and deciding set at the Wimbledon tennis tournament. If TZP is in fact an involuntary, unconscious, state of being, **then this incident was like two people dreaming the same dream at the same time, battling for control of the drama and its outcome. "This is my world"— "no, it's mine...".**

Well, they proceeded to give the world of spectators a rare look into The Zone, as that last set went on for an exhausting 11 hours and five minutes. If you saw that match, you are smiling right now just thinking about it. If you didn't see or hear about it, you are probably also smiling in anticipation of hearing the details. Both players exhibited a level of mental and physical performance that exceeded even their own expectations, as the epic marathon battle went on and on and on.

We will examine this event in *Keys to the City,* and gleam more from what it reveals about The Zone Phenomena and human potential. Suffice it for now to say, that both players had to produce exceptional offense, defense, and stamina, to wage a battle that stretched into three consecutive days.

$\sim$

Another example of the rare phenomenon of two players experiencing The Zone at the same time was the 1998 Major

League Baseball *"Home Run Race"*—the season long marathon battle between eventual winner Mark McGwire and runner-up Sammy Sosa[3]. That slugfest inspired this poem:

THE GREAT HOME RUN RACE

37 years and it stood the test of time
A monument to greatness, a mountain to climb.
Two years before the millennium,
two worriers emerge,
A battle is waged...with haste they converge.
Long ball after long ball...the greatest head to head,
The fans are all captivated...our appetites are fed.
And when the dust settled the old record was dead.
All hail to the king as he sits on his throne
Like the sweet song of the red bird,
May these heroes live long.

©2012 jw

That epic battle would have likely produced even more home runs if those two sluggers were not intentionally walked so many times. The world came out in droves to view this historic spectacle—as is the case with all public displays of human transcendence.

Tarnished History?

To answer those who believe this history is tarnished by accusations of steroid use in major league baseball: I will say again: this book is about human transcendence, and the potential hidden by normality—that human potential which causes what is normal to become mediocre in its shadow. That "potential" has to *reside there to begin with*, before it can be

---

[3] See video here: http://bit.ly/1elS69Y

released. We are not talking about discovering a new species, but maximizing the performance of what already exists.

It appears to me that no pill has yet to be found with the ability to produce TZP level of brain performance. If it had, *everyone* would want it. We know strength and endurance can be *enhanced* through nutritional and pharmaceutical supplementation.

Notably, only two baseball players entered The Zone of transcendence during the 1998 home run race, although—we have it on good authority—many used performance enhancing drugs.

The question as to whether drugs introduce something foreign and super natural, or merely enhance/unleash what is already there, has not definitively been answered to my knowledge. If health was no concern, and every opponent was ferocious; how many of us then, would supplement to improve our mental or physical performance?

That's as far as I can go for now on the controversial aspects of that great season, but it stands in my mind to be a legitimate manifestation of TZP's awesome power over two competitors at the same time. (More on this in chapter 7.)

We will meet many more transient residents on the road to The Zone as we move on.

CHAPTER THREE

The Power Source

*"...Tapping both sides of the brain,
resulting in complete control of one's own body, rapid
processing of new and stored information,undisturbed
concentration, extraordinary performance "*
—jw

We will examine the permanent inhabitants of The Zone in a bit; but for now let's answer these questions: How does this phenomenon occur? What is its power source? Like the heart beat to life, what animates the super high performing inhabitants of The Zone?

THE BRAIN THE SOURCE

It's easy to start with the brain because all of our life experiences are controlled and managed by our brains. It is the filter through which our interactions with life are processed—from the insignificant to the phenomenal.

We are considering something beyond the natural, material, common, easy to comprehend things of life. For example, the brain is responsible for (to exactly what extent we may never know) our thoughts and emotions, which are intangible and usually associate with the mind. We know that the physical brain is involved, because our thoughts and emotions can be affected by drugs. For example: drugs can make you happy, uninhibited, depressed, aggressive, delusional etc. This fact that the brain doesn't just control physical things is certain to nudge us beyond the realm of natural things into the super-natural.

It is not my intention to try to completely explain the supernatural or spiritual aspects of the brain. Since the science is still new, I prefer to stay away from filling in the gaps with fantasy and imagination—which is hard not to do when contemplating the brain. Many popular books on the subject do just that, and because no one knows better, the expert is allowed to draw all kinds of fantastic conclusions. We will, on the other hand, explore some solid facts related to the brain's role in The Zone. I will offer my own impressions and thoughts...then let you draw your own conclusions and spiritual implications.

PROCESSING POWER

Let's appreciate the power it takes to produce the extraordinary feats we witness in The Zone, and the source of that power.

The Mighty Brain Cell

The cell is the basic building block of life. All forms of life (plant, animal, human) are comprised of specialized cells which come together to form the internal and visible components of each form of life. If you break down the human body for example, to its least common denominator, you will arrive at the cell. (Later, in the chapter on Heredity we will divide the cell further).

Each organ and part of the body has its own type of cell: eye cells, brain cells (neurons), skin cells, bone cell, hair, etc. Each cell is an incredible, miniscule, complicated, and surpassingly intelligent, self-contained manufacturing facility that does its special part for the human body and being. It is a production facility where the biological human being begins the physical process of coming into maturity, and by which it is maintained.

It is fascinating to contemplate, that from one single cell, the body becomes an amalgamation of trillions of cells. Each, at the right point in the dividing process became a specialized contributor to the whole living being.

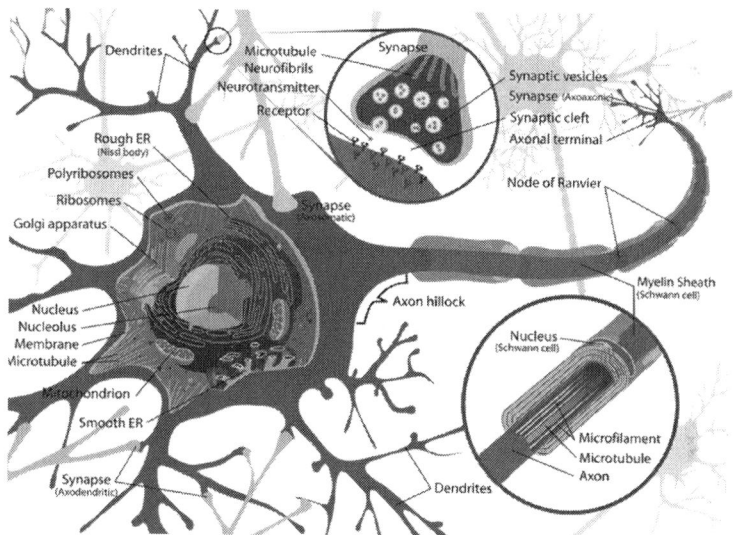

Brain cell, smaller than a grain of sand. htp://commons.wikimedia. org/wiki/File:Complete_neuron_cell_diagram_en.svg

Well, at the right time, our brain cells began to divide and specialize into their proper place and function. This process is so automatic and involuntary, we are likely to take it for granted. (Forgive me for frequently using this phrase, but this book is not about anything new, it's about phenomena we have in fact taken for granted, overlooked, or minimized.)

I want you to focus on the fact that the phenomenon of human transcendence begins at the start of our development. We are in every conceivable aspect phenomenal—every one of us. When the female egg cell and the male sperm cell combine into a single new cell, the phenomenon of a new human being is rapidly underway. That single cell with its internal instructions begins to divide, and divide, 2, 4, 8, 16, and so on, until we have a human being with all of the parts and functions necessary for life on earth.

Cells let in nutrients (which it turns into useful chemicals), and expels waste while preventing anything harmful from entering (security)—pure genius. Enzymes in the cells are the molecules that turn water and food into chemicals for that cell and other parts of the body to use. A single cell can contain a large number of enzymes: there are 40,000-75,000 different enzymes inside human cells. That means at least 40,000 different chemical reactions.[1] Are you getting the picture of incredible activity at the core of our bodies? We are talking about a cell so small you can fit about 5000 of the smallest on the head of a pin. The neuron cell body, (diagram on previous page,) not unlike all other cells, is estimated to be 1/200 to 1/10 of a millimeter in size (a grain of sand is much larger: approximately 1/16 mm in size). Talk about miniature high-tech marvels. What happens when that marvel is multiplied?

Nuclear Power

I called the cell "the least common denominator" of the human body, but that is not exactly true, because inside the cell

---

[1] http://www.biologymad.com/master.html?http://www.biologymad.com/enzymes/enzymes.htm

is where the real phenomenon of physical life resides. Take a look again at the brain cell drawing on the previous page, and notice all the labels marking some of the individual parts of the cell. Each of those parts has an important specialized function; so important, each could be designated the least common denominator.

Notice the very small dot in the center of that cell? That's the "nucleus," which contains the DNA molecule, which contains the genetic code (encyclopedia of blue print instructions) for the entire human body.

As we move through this process of discovering our maximum performance potential, and tapping into it, we need to remember what we have to work with—the capable, dedicated, and specialized parts, which make up *us* human beings, all contributing to our potential.

Another important point I want to highlight here is how *involuntary* or *unconscious* we are in this process. It is a fact, that in the process of our development and ultimate potential, we are mostly passive. The *program* unfolds, and we generally respond to it with the highest form of intelligence that it provides us. If this is the case, we are more likely to perform at peak potential if we are cooperating with the intelligent program, and less likely to, if we are working against the program. **In TZP this cooperation becomes forced and automatic, to the extent that the whole body is working in perfect harmony.** From conception to adult maturity, this intelligence (in such a magnificently unfolding program), does a fabulous job all on its own.

Its program is flawless; our own conscious efforts have proven comparatively flawed and inconsistent, and therefore unreliable. (There is no such thing as absolute perfection among the *deeds* of men. There are always flaws to be found—often glaring ones). I will prove this point in chapter 7, when we consider roadblocks and such—many of which are self-imposed. If conscious control produces mediocrity, and unconscious (The Zone) produces near perfection, then we may logically ask: if we tap in to this flawless system, will that perfection spill out into normal life? In *The Zone Phenomenon,* it does!

∾

Neuroscientists estimate we are born with around *100 billion* brain cells (neurons). Let's not just walk past a humongous number like this—that figuratively reaches from earth past the moon—and fail to gawk at it. If you were to count just 1 billion of these 100 billion tiny marvels, counting nonstop day and night, it would take you about 95 years to finish the task. It would take 99 generations of your family (if one offspring picked up the task) to finish counting all of the neurons in your brain. Counting every ticking second of the clock would take 3,100 years just to arrive at 100 billion seconds.[2]

Our *entire* nervous system contains an estimated *1,000 billion* neurons. When we remember how small, complex, and powerful they are, the number of them becomes even more incredible.

Did you know that no two of your 100,000,000,000 (100 billion, or one hundred thousand million) brain cells are exactly alike? That's right! Each one is different in shape from the others. This staggering fact indicates *specialization* and *diversity* (principles you will hear more of later) within our

---

[2] http://www.squidoo.com/how-much-is-a-trillion

brain's crowded neural community. Add to this, the fact that brain cells do not regenerate...if one dies it is not replaced, like a skin cell for example. This fact adds to diversity and specialization, the principle of **deliberate purpose** for each cell—each one has a unique and specific task to accomplish.

Neurogenesis?

Let me interrupt myself to address the recently popular theory of neurogenesis: the theory that new brain cells can be created in a mature adult. This of course contradicts the long held belief (which I've just re-asserted in the last paragraph) that adults can only loose brain cells, they do not produce any new ones.

The idea of neurogenesis is marketed by a few self help gurus as scientific proof that you can easily create a "new brain" by applying certain principles, and effectively change your life for the better.

One of the strongest arguments against this view (aside from the lack of physical evidence demonstrating neurogenesis in aging adult human beings), is given in an article on Neurophilosophy titled *Does your brain produce new cells? A skeptical view of human adult neurogenesis,* by Mo Costandi, hosted by The Guardian:

> "One side-effect of having a large and complex brain is that you wouldn't want naïve newcomers barging in," says Lumsden. "How would new neurons usefully integrate into complex neural networks? If anything, evolution would have made damn sure that mechanisms exist to eliminate these party-crashers."[3]

---

[3] http://alturl.com/ks3zn ;This short article is worth reading for a very clear view of the debate on neurogenesis.

POWER SURGE

Each of those 100 billion specialized neurons are capable of communicating with 10-15 thousand other neurons[4]...resulting in trillions (thousands of billions) of instructions, signals, messages, and commands being sent at any given time within our brain and nervous system. Trillions!

One estimate has **one billion** grains of sand needing 43 one gallon milk jugs to contain them. If the neurons in our brain were the size of grains of sand, it would take 4,300 milk jugs to contain them. It's ok to visualize—if you can—4,300 milk jugs stuffed with sand-sized neurons. So then, just **one trillion** grains of sand would need 43,000 milk jugs. Each single grain, would represent a single bit of important information being shared between neurons within the brain and nervous system. But 43,000 jugs aren't enough because we are talking about **trillions** (with an "s") of neural connections. This is staggering, incomprehensible synchronicity, cooperation, communication, power, and potential, situated between our ears—unequaled anywhere on earth. This is "control central" for the highest form of life, consciousness, and function on planet earth—us!

If the seven billion people on planet earth all joined hands, like neurons, to accomplish a single task, that monumental cooperation would need to be multiplied a thousand times to equal the powerful connections between our neurons. Every neuron working together for the execution of a single purpose; each providing essential input for the completion of the task—1,000 billion of them! The brain is one powerful organ!

---

[4] The Wonder of Man, Werner Gitt, director and professor at the German Federal Institute of Physics and Technology

When comparing the brain with other complex life forms in our world its awesome ability can't be exaggerated.

"During the development of the organism from a fertilized ovum, neurons are formed at the astounding rate of 250,000 per minute over nine months."
- Dr. Werner Gitt, *The Wonder Of Man*

From the time the brain is developed in the womb, and begins to receive, process, and send signals to the rest of our body, it processes and manages an incomprehensible amount of tasks **to perfection**. After birth our brains are busy. Well, that's an understatement. It is managing the development of that newborn, executing pre-programmed instructions, receiving information from the four senses, analyzing, processing, storing, adapting, teaching, instructing, guiding, etc.

By the way, there is good reason to believe that the cell itself has a super high level of intelligence, not only in its DNA, but in other areas of its structure (which are duplicated and passed on to its offspring every time the cell divides). Mitochondria (the cells amazing, motorized power generators), for example, have their own DNA code. So then, the genetic code—inside the nucleus—is not *solely* responsible for the body's development and maintenance, other cell components contribute, but that's for another remarkable discussion.

Our brain plays a critical role in every single function and process within our body and out through our extremities (arms, hands, feet, legs etc.). It's no small thing to regulate heart beat, breathing, blood circulation, body temperature, eyesight, hearing, balance, immune function etc., and still manage physical performance at the highest level; making it appear so effortless we take it for granted—*until* we lose some ability.

Scientists say, that the heart is a phenomenal workhorse, but it has a few tasks, whereas the brain has too many tasks to number...and it too must perform for a lifetime. As the manager and supervisor of all of our body functions and systems, it is hands down the body's workhorse.

NEURAL NETWORK: THE POWER GRID

Let's turn our attention to another aspect of the brains power—energy! Electrical energy that is generated as the 100,000 million neurons inside of our brain and nervous system communicate with each other. Can you fathom each single neuron simultaneously communicating by way of electrical and biochemical messages with 10,000 other cells?

Remember, each single cell is a self contained intelligent information generating and processing facility. Imagine yourself as a business person with a network of 10,000 associates, at your instantaneous command, committed to making you a success. How much power and potential would that represent? Well, each of the 100 thousand million neurons has at least that many connections in its network, serving your every command. Life appears so easy it's hard to wrap our minds around such raw power and potential.

Hopefully, the power of TZP is beginning to come into clearer focus

> "The brain can do 10^{18} = 1 million million million computations **in a second**, which is a hundred million times as fast as the fastest super computer at time of writing (10^{10} calculations per second). The most

fascinating aspect, however, is not the actual physical performance of the brain, but its ability to process these unimaginably vast quantities of information in unique ways which we cannot yet fully comprehend."
—**Werner Gitt**, *The Wonder of Man*

If we were able to see this activity, what would it look like? Most drawings that illustrate our neural circuitry depict small bursts of electrical light at the synapses, (where neurons connect or transfer information to each other). But, that doesn't do justice to the phenomenon. In reality, those bursts of electrical energy are on top each other. When you think of 100, thousand million sparks multiplied 10,000 times, we get the picture of an amazing radiant glow of electrical energy.

Remember the illustration of the gallon milk jugs— 43,000 of them? Thankfully, neurons are infinitely smaller then grains of sand (or we'd have really huge heads)—to the extent 100 billion can easily fit into the area of our brain, with plenty of room for millions of other important cells. Nevertheless, the cluster of neurons is very densely packed. If we didn't know better, we could think them to be haphazardly stuffed or crammed into the skull.

Without the skin that covers our skeleton, and if our muscle tissue were transparent, we would look like some kind of glowing extra-terrestrial being, as these sparks constantly ignite.

This magnificent energy production is a reality within our bodies every millisecond of our lives. It is the power that animates us. We don't usually think about the electrical side of our bodies until the old ticker (heart) fails, and needs to be jump started with the booster cables—clear!

RAPID PROCESSING

This brings us to my favorite aspect of The Zone Phenomenon, which I call "rapid processing." My original theory on
the dynamics of TZP states:

> "The Zone is a state of being carried along by a
> CrunchTime induced hypnosis, that taps both sides of
> the brain. Resulting in complete control over one's own
> body, rapid processing of new and stored information,
> undisturbed concentration, prolific scoring."

©2011, J.W.W.J.

Previously, I introduced the former pro baseball player
Lem P. The experience he shared with me, combined with my
fascination with the world's love affair with sports (to the extent of religious fanaticism), led me to write quite a few poems
like "Studies in the So-Called Zone"™ (above).

Lem shared experiencing the sensation of the baseball
coming at him (from the pitcher) in slow motion. As a matter of fact, the entire scene, as I recall, was experienced in
what felt to him like slow motion. This sensation is common
among those who have experienced and shared their Zone
visit. When I had the experience (I shared earlier) during a
round of golf, I had a similar feeling. Because the action is
much slower in golf compared to baseball, I believe the sensation was not as dramatic; but was closer to being in a subtle
trance that kept me from being distracted by conversations
with my playing partners or anything else happening around
me.

Recently, an acquaintance shared experiencing TZP four
times during his former baseball days, and once while work-

ing as a dispatcher. On the latter occasion, he was able to handle a very high volume of calls coming in, and resolve every problem effortlessly over a period of hours. As he told his story I envisioned an octopus moving at blurring speed.

Because the *feelings* were the same on all occasions, he recognized them as the same phenomenon. The experience never happened again on that job. It is as though he was allowed to enter The Zone on a limited number of occasions. Although I would say, receiving four or five temporary passes to The Zone region is very fortunate for any transient.

Professional athletes share that similar, almost identical experience. Annika Sorenstam, when asked about the day she shot the lowest score ever on the Ladies Professional Golf Tour said:

> *"I remember the start because it was just so incredible. I birdied the first eight holes. The shots weren't really that great, but it was just the flow to it all and the momentum just kept building and building. I could do nothing wrong that day. Everything funneled to the green. Every putt had the right pace."*[5]

When asked directly by Dave Allen (her interviewer) to describe what it felt like to be *in The Zone*, she shared:

> *"First of all, it feels effortless. You don't think about hazards. You think about fairways and greens. When you putt, you see a big hole. You see the line. You don't question your decisions...."*

You'll notice by her description that she did not attribute

the experience to an act of her will—it was in her words "just the flow, the momentum kept building." That sounds a lot like being carried along by something, involuntarily. She was aware, but not in conscious control. Some may say that she was in total control, because her every wish was accomplished. But that is the nature of TZP...wishes are effortlessly granted— for a time. Give credit where it is due. If I didn't directly cause it, it's a gift, not an effect which I intentionally caused.

I recall another interview in which Annika stated her sister walked behind her—after it became apparent she was in The Zone—so as not to interfere with the mental state she was in. (More on this detail in "Roadblocks...")

In a CNN interview she states:

> *"Really what happened is it felt so easy I wasn't really thinking and every putt I hit just went in. I never really thought about a second putt, it just went in, and I went off to the next hole. It was one of those days when there was no effort and things just went my way."*[6]

I'm pretty sure if asked if she felt like she was in a type of trance, she would say yes.

Where Does This Sensation Come From?

What exactly is happening? These are the type of questions we need to answer.

I have described this aspect of the phenomenon as ***"rapid processing of new and stored information"*** because this is precisely what is occurring in The Zone experience. Earlier I said, watching Michael Jordan was probably my first recollec-

---

[6] http://edition.cnn.com/2006/SPORT/golf/09/06/sorenstam.interview/index.html

tion of being impressed with, what I perceived to be TZP. He appeared to defy gravity, out maneuver opponents, keep his balance, and score the shot, while time stood still.

It was obvious to me that Jordan was rapidly processing all of the variable information he encountered on the way to the basket much faster than his opponents, or even the fans could anticipate. He was *thinking fast*—but it had to be even more than that—because the action required more than fast thinking.

Certainly through practice a player can learn to anticipate the reactions of a defender or two, (the playbook and film review are designed to help predict opponents reactions). But many of Jordan's feats, over and between several defenders, were clearly beyond that; He would elevate, adjust his body mid-air, slicing, and twisting with ease, patience, and grace. This was possible, I believe, because his brain was processing at a super fast rate, with such ease, that made him *comfortable* while simultaneously analyzing all of his options, and finally gracefully scoring the lay-up, jump shot, assist, or dunk.

For this to happen his brain had to process the **new information** it was receiving—on the fly—from his senses, especially sight and hearing; as well as **stored information** from practice, study, and experience. **His brain had to analyze, process, prioritize, predict, calculate, utilize, or dismiss all of this information, and direct his body to respond in a matter of seconds or less.** The action is dynamic; decisions have to be made one after another, split second by split second. In the event two or more defenders are converging, the decisions may arrive on top of each other.

As we have seen, this is no big deal for the brain, because

it is constantly processing at a super high level of speed and proficiency, behind the scene. **The Zone Phenomenon apparently brings what is normally hidden of the brain's super power, out into the open for a brief moment in time for all to behold.**

Jordan's seemingly effortless, controlled grace, in such a chaotic situation, contrasted with other players I've studied, highlights the power of The Zone to *slow down the action* in the perception of the person under its influence.

～

Another example of this dynamic in sports was seen in the great professional football running back, Barry Sanders. Now, there have been several professional running backs to transcend the bounds of human performance out of the backfield, like Jim Brown and Earl Campbell. But these guys have usually done it by running over and through their opponents. I will by no means minimize such a display of raw power and brute force in trampling and pulverizing opponents; but what Sanders did required a different set of exceptional skills.

Barry Sanders was respected and feared because of the grace and finesse by which he dominated opponents on the football field. Few professional running backs—if any—have shown this ability. Sanders exhibited Zone-level *rapid processing* of information as he (at only 5'8" tall) chose not to power over opponents, but to out-wit and out-maneuver them. One defensive linebacker said he even saw Barry Sanders divide in two pieces: Pointing at the replay screen he swore he saw Sanders' body double.

Barry said of his strategy: "I don't think, I just react". I interpret this as, not restricting the brain by predicting the future, but allowing the brain to respond to the action with its on-the-fly super fast processing ability. Like a tap dancer, he would elude defenders, shaking and faking would-be tacklers as he danced his way into the record books. Rapid brain processing of TZP allowed him to regularly react with apparent control and grace in the unpredictable, chaotic, and fast-paced environment on the field...Calculating paths over or around when time would seemingly allow only the option of over or through the defenders.

A brief note: I know there is a very thin line between great talent and The Zone Phenomenon—we will discuss talent later—in the meantime you can form your own conclusions about the source of these exceptional performers' abilities.

Approaching the Waterfall

I believe it is the brains' focusing a large portion of its *one million, million, million calculations a second* on the task at hand—while at the same time relegating all lesser priority activities to secondary status—that creates the **trance like, slow-motion, sleep walking, unconscious sensation** experienced in The Zone.

While in the realm of TZP, you are very aware of other things going on—with and around you—but the brain is not *focused* on them, so they receive only peripheral attention. Like a daydream they are a part of the background scenery... muffled sounds...the atmosphere...they are extras in the movie, filling-out the scene while the camera focuses on the leading character.

Meanwhile, more brain power and resources of *the trillions* are devoted to the task at hand, in what I perceive as *"rapid processing: from a rushing river to a waterfall of information"*—like a drop in a bucket—with tremendous proficiency and ease. If the average athlete engaged in competition experiences a fast moving stream, then the subject of TZP experiences "the waterfall" of information processing—a literal torrential rain, as the natural aqueducts of information and processing reserves are opened from beneath or—more correctly—from within.

∽

I recall an incident of sleepwalking when I was around 10 years old. I remember standing on the corner of my street after having jumped out of my sister's first floor bedroom window in the middle of the night. Don't laugh, this could happen to anyone—right?

My strongest memory was the sensations of the sounds and sights of the cars and headlights whizzing by on the major street a block away. It appears—in hindsight—as though the super proficient brain processing that goes on during the sleep phase had continued while I was partially awake, and produced a sense of blurred sound and motion from my surroundings. If the brain is moving super fast, everything else would appear slow. I will share more on this concept shortly.

The explanation here may also provide an understanding for the "Déjà Vu" ("I've experienced this before") phenomenon. Both phenomena are obviously a heightened brain state —as is the dream state itself—where the brain has sole control of the entire body without distractions from conscious life. Which also explains why Zone residents experience a "sleep walking" feeling.

~

Now, back to this torrential waterfall of information processing.

I stumbled onto the phrase "rapid processing", and it is a perfect description of what occurs in the brain during The Zone Phenomenon.

> ***Rapid***: *taken from realm of moving water, is defined as "An increase in velocity or turbulence, somewhere between a smooth flowing stream and a waterfall."*

All of these characteristics are present when the brain has entered The Zone.

If our normal condition can be described as a smooth flowing stream; we progress from there, through "a rapid" toward "a waterfall" the more powerful our Zone experience. Our brain under normal everyday circumstances is supervising an incredible amount of information and tasks (as we have seen), which could conservatively be called a waterfall, but take that state, concentrate it, and multiply it by five, 10, or more (who knows), and you have The Zone Phenomenon.

Or, better yet—take the one million, million, million calculations per second, occurring at 250 mph between neurons, and bring it into a conscious 2 mph[7] (normal awake state) environment...Add to this, a conscious awareness at the same blazing speed...equally proficient eye-hand coordination... and you have...

---

[7] Estimate Only

The Matrix-Like Slow-Motion

I can't help but be reminded of a scene in *The Matrix*™ movie. The main character "Neo" reaching a higher level of perception, awareness, and ability, causing a slow-motion effect as bullets are coming at him in super fast real-time. But, his brain is way ahead of the action, processing beyond super fast, causing the super fast to appear as super slow-motion.

Is this what Lem P., the former pro baseball player, and other athletes are talking about when they say things like: "I could count the stitches on the 95 mile per hour fast ball as it was coming at me in what seemed like slow motion?" Or "The crowd and the noise were muffled, and the baseball looked the size of a cantaloupe?"

In that situation the brains main task was to knock the cover off the baseball, so it focused like a laser beam on that objective. Drawing from the reserves of knowledge, training, and experience, while focusing the senses, the brain was able to calculate at a rate much faster than the approaching ball—calculating speed, size, path, estimated time of arrival, etc. Thus, creating the "slow motion," cantaloupe-sized baseball sensation, as the slow moving 95 mph spheroid approached. Having not abdicated its primary life sustaining responsibilities, the brain continued to monitor and manage all of the senses, creating a definite—although muted—awareness of the surroundings, including the boisterous fans.

The Man Who Sees In Slow Motion

In 2002 a man named Jason Padgett was brutally mugged and received a concussion (brain trauma). Shortly after recovering, he became an "acquired Savant" with genius level math and artistic ability.

Jason said, after his head injury "reality lost its smoothness." When he explained exactly what he means, he appears to confirm my hypothesis that *the brain's internal super performance* **comes out** *into normal life.* He says, concerning his new perception of reality, that a car driving along smoothly, now becomes a scene played out in separate frames like the old cartoon flip book drawings: one frame at a time coming together to simulate motion.

If I interpret him correctly—he now sees action in slow motion. His brain processing is so fast, it splits seconds into fragments...and he is consciously aware of it. If there was not video to verify this, it would be difficult to believe. *(Watch a video of Jason on my blog[8]).* I don't know the science behind high speed cameras used to capture fast action (such as in sports), a thousands of frames per second, but Jason's eyes and brain now have the capability to see much faster than normal sight. This is his new *everyday experience*—latent brain potential uncovered by accident.

Speed is Relative in The Zone

To help further illustrate this phenomenon, I'll use terms we may be able to more easily grasp. Assume there is a person walking along a busy side walk at normal speed (3 miles per hour). She is passed by a cyclist, biking at about 15 mph. To the cyclist, the walker is moving pretty slowly. A car, traveling at 35 mph, passes them both. To the person walking and the cyclist, the car is moving very fast. On the freeway overpass,

---

[8] http://goo.gl/ZlT83h

cars zoom by at 65 mph. Just to the left, a 747 jet plane is taking off into the air at 180 mph. To those looking out of the window of the 747, every moving thing below them appears to be barely moving—including the cars on the freeway.

During The Zone Phenomenon, your brain is in the 747 at cruising speed of 564 mph; everything else on planet earth is moving in slow-motion by comparison.

The Eye

The avalanche of information that the brain processes—especially during intense "in The Zone" performance—is incredible if only we consider what it processes through just one of the body's five senses,

For example, the amount of information the brain receives, interprets, and processes from the eye alone is staggering. Furthermore, when it comes to athletic performance sight is typically relied upon more than any other sense. If we were considering music performance, the same could be said about the ear.

Oracle's® ThinkQuest, Computer vs. Brain website,[9] considering the brains performance ability states:

*"At the same time, the brain is constantly bombarded by all your senses all at once. **In one mere second,** the retina sends **ten one-million-point images** to the brain. At the same time, your ear drums pass sound information real-time at higher-than-CD-quality. And don't forget the information sent to the brain by your sense of touch and smell. If a normal higher-end computer was fed with the information from a human's senses constantly and asked to process and react to them, the computer would overload from too much*

---

9 http://library.thinkquest.org/C001501/the_saga/compare.htm

information because it can't react as fast as the brain could."

The same kinds of conclusions are reached by every scientist who studies the brain and/or the human nervous system in general. As a matter of fact, I was surprised in my research to find several scientists who have been led to beliefs of a spiritual nature as a result of their work and studies on the human brain and nervous system. It is truly an amazing system.

The "10 one-million-point images" sent from the eye to the brain per second are enough to require the brain to process a *Niagara Falls* volume of information in a blink—and incredibly it does. Not only does it, but it does it with ease and proficiency, so much so, that we take it for granted.

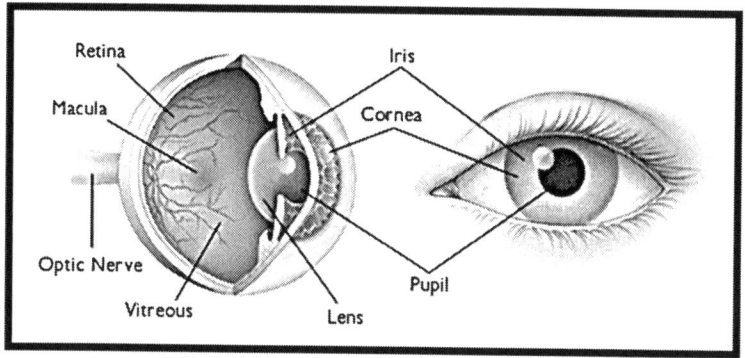

Drawing of the eye, our visual information receptor and processor.

When the parts of the eye and their special functions are broken down, we are able to divide the process of seeing into the various steps it takes. The iris controls the amount of incoming light (all sight is light rays); the lens focuses the light on the retina for processing,; the rods and cones (100 million of them!) convert the image information into chemicals, then electrical signals, and send them via the optical nerve to the brain for final processing, interpretation, and action. Double that if you have two functioning eyes.

It takes time for us to describe the process, but the eye processes 10 one-million-point bits of visual information in a second. Divide that into fragments of time if you can! It is occurring as we speak—if you have your sight. It does take time, but at a speed far beyond our normal comprehension.

When we combine what the brain *receives* in one second from the eyes during athletic performance, with what it *retrieves* from the storage files of training, learning, and memory, with what it *directs* our body to do in response; the image of a waterfall of information processing becomes more convincing, accurate, vivid, and incredible. This is the source and cause of the Matrix-like slow-motion effect experienced by the inhabitants of The Zone. **What is normally experienced in comfortable ticking seconds is sucked-up quickly in accelerated fractions of seconds in TZP.**

Now, let's see more of this power in action as it reaches *full potential* in those individuals who like Jason Padgett *live* in The Zone 24/7.

CHAPTER FOUR

The Citizens: Permanent Residents Of The Zone

"Maximum sustained human performance"
—*jw*

A fter witnessing the tremendous energy, power, and potential, produced by the brain's network of 100 billion neurons and their trillions of connections, it should be easy to appreciate the *temporary* Zone experience. We know that TZP briefly *maximizes* brain and body performance. Therefore we understand the *need*—after such an exhaustively demanding Zone excursion—to return to the steady normal pace of ordinary life. This need is the same as needing rest after all of your brain power and energy have been devoted to studying for an important test. Or needing to rest after lifting an automobile to save a family member. Your energies have been concentrated like a laser beam on a certain task, and now the tension needs to be relieved, and the body allowed to rest and recuperate.

You will learn as our journey continues: that this is exactly the type of intense power our body generates to create TZP. Can anything run full throttle continually? So, the idea of *temporary* visits to The Zone is understandable.

But, it is very hard to understand how anyone can operate under such intense mental and physical power on a daily, minute by minute basis. Remember, **The Zone is a maximum human performance state**. As we will see later, the stress hormone adrenaline is involved in most Zone experiences—certainly where physical strength is necessary.

So then, the idea of "permanent" residents of The Zone seems a thing of comic book fiction. Even Superman and The Hulk had to return to normal life after a period of super performance. Compared to normal human performance, this would be like expecting Babe Ruth to have hit a home run every time at bat...or every painting by Michelangelo to have been as captivating as the Mona Lisa...Kobe Bryant to score 50 points every game. It just doesn't happen but for brief periods of Zone-induced perfection.

So then, how do I include this category of *permanent residents* of The Zone?

TRUE HUMAN POTENTIAL

PRODIGY - MASTER OF MATHEMATICS: Matt Savage taught himself to play the piano over night after "solving the logic of the piano's 88 keys."

I'm not a musician, but I have some idea of what that type of feat by an untrained novice entails. He would not only have to quickly understand every note's relationship to every other note, but the logic of the order of the piano keys, and their harmonies, as well as connect that head knowledge with the hands and fingertips...to name a few.

Matt was diagnosed as "deeply Autistic." At the age of six, Matt told his mother his *head was filled with mathematical problems.* He was diagnosed with "Hyperlexia" (initially identified by Silberg and Silberg (1967), who defined it as the precocious (gifted) ability to read words without prior training and learning; to read, (typically) before the age of 5.[1]

(This helps build my case for "involuntary privilege".) The *"Rain Man,"* who was also autistic, demonstrated this same ability: his father doesn't know how he learned to read. **This ability to read words without being taught is unbelievable —if it were not true.** Think about some 4 year old you know suddenly reading words out loud; you would be shocked to say the least.

We are now traveling further into this remarkable district.

A Glimpse Into The Heart of The Zone

I personally believe there's a natural connection between language, math, and music, at a fundamental level—like the connection between gravity and flight, or peanut butter and jelly (I'm joking about the latter). We appreciate this connection in music and poetry: the elegant written word, where words.—their sound—their meaning—.come together with mathematical logic—in cadence, tone, inflection and rhythm, to produce a universally appreciated pleasant musical sound. Just a glimpse for now—a closer look soon.

---

[1] http://en.wikipedia.org/wiki/Hyperlexia

The Home Run Machine *He's not a man. He's a machine. Synchronized the eye, the hand, the hand, the eye. He thinks, he sees, faster than sound the crack of the bat...More brilliant than the sun...Another home run. –Joe Walker*

The young music genius may not understand the principles of mathematics outside the realm of music, but instinctively understands its logic in relation to sound, beats, melody and harmony. In Savage's case, his intimate knowledge of math was combined with an ear for music to produce his incredible performance.

Matt Savage's incredible music and math ability as a child certainly puts him in The Zone as a resident. But, a question arises: do we classify him and other prodigies as temporary or permanent residents? Their residency in The Zone region is certainly lengthy, (no fleeting daydream type of experience), but is it permanent? Many studies and biographies reveal, the gap between the prodigy and their same age peers narrows significantly with age, and some become normal, or high performing adults, but nothing like the transcendent perfor-mance they exhibited for their age as children.

Savage is typical of child prodigies who transcend normal human performance for an extended residence in The Zone. But we've only glimpsed the **sustained power** of The Zone on an individual.

SAVANTS

What we witness of The Zone in athletic performance, and many child prodigies, is unfortunately a *peek* into the realm of real brain power—a mere slice of the pie of which the savant gets a much larger portion. The athlete who performs in The Zone on frequent or extended occasions still has to eventually succumb to injury and age. The prodigy, as we will see, often settles into normality. Both face *inevitable eviction* from The Zone.

Savants however, have *permanent residence* to the region. Savants are people who have extraordinary abilities in certain areas such as music, art, science, and math. (You've already met Jason Padgett who acquired savant performance later in life after being beaten.) They are—you could say—among few categories of permanent residents, and everyone else is a transient.

The point that I want to emphasize is: there are human beings like you and me, with brains like ours, who are processing information, and functioning on a Zone kind of level 24/7. **This reality can't be ignored!**

However, we will discover that *sustaining* such a high level of brain performance is not easy—even for the privileged permanent residents of The Zone. Some type of "short circuit" or "power failure" is very likely. If the average athlete engaged in competition, experiences a fast-flowing stream...then the savant experiences "the waterfall" of information processing and performance—*all the time.*

Although savants demonstrate weaknesses and limitations in some areas of functionality, they *always* demonstrate supernatural ability in at least one area of knowledge and performance. It is therefore logical to look to their mental abilities as proof of greater brain and performance potential in all human beings.

Without further ado, let's meet more of these rare *citizens* of The Zone State.

~

Pure Brain Power: Daniel Tamment, the man featured in such documentaries as the Science Channel's *Brain Man,* known as a prodigious savant, has what appears to be a perfect ability to calculate complex math equations in his head at the speed of a calculator. As a matter of fact, he normally outperforms the calculator on speed and number of decimal places.

Stay with me here—I said he normally outperforms the calculator! Who's "numeral uno" on planet earth, man or machine?

Like every other savant, Tamment has an incredible memory, which he put to the test by accepting a challenge to recite the infinite number "pi." Tamment was allowed to read the numbers once, then, in the presence of five mathematicians with the correct numbers in front of them, he recited the first **22,000 digits** of pi...from memory! It took over five hours to finish. That's five hours of 7, 3, 0, 5, 1, 8...and on...and on...one digit after another, without one single mistake. This is pure inexplicable brain power at work (see video on my blog)[2].

Before you think this has to involve some type of super natural force (clairvoyant, possession, etc.); other men have accomplished the same feat, but they studied for days and

---

[2] http://un-conscious.com

weeks before succeeding—very impressive all the same. This is extraordinary memory; maximum brain performance.

Daniel read the 22,000 + digit number once! I could not come close to reciting the first 20 digits of pie, and that would probably take me several days of study. Anyway you look at this kind of feat, it is truly transcendent—beyond our realm of normality. And it speaks of latent human potential.

Behold The Zone!

Daniel is also able to calculate complex math problems at lightning speed; so his gift is more than a powerful memory.

Question: Is Tamment a "have", and the rest of us "have-nots?" We must eventually answer this question. Stay with me.

Daniel Tamment is a rare savant, because he is able to function in the world and communicate effectively like most other human beings, while most savants are limited (by crippling "autistic" traits) in everyday tasks such as interpersonal relationships, and simple tasks like dressing themselves.

How Does Daniel Do It?

As I see it, we have two options when it comes to explaining how savants like Tamment are able to calculate complex equations almost instantly. The first is purely spiritual: These savants are endowed with a spiritual insight that is given on the fly as needed—that is, when you ask Tamment what 98 to the 5th power is, he is shown by unseen forces, or the answer is placed in his mind, and he in turn speaks it. Many, like Tamment, say they do not calculate, they just know or see the answer. That's right, he is adamant about the fact that he doesn't consciously calculate the answers.

The other option is: his brain calculates the answer in a

manner and speed that he is consciously unaware of, and he in turn speaks the answer, which—by the way—is *always* correct. This is closer to the way Tamment explains his ability. He sees the answer as shapes and colors, which represent certain numbers. He knows what number each color and shape stand for. Don't ask me who taught him that, or how he knows this. Let's try to keep some kind of stable footing here...not everything can be explained.

Although, we do know that it's possible to have a brain that performs at a speed much faster than normal conscious experience: We saw this in Padgett, who sees motion at a super high speed camera rate. Perhaps Daniel's brain performs the same when it comes to mathematics.

Similarly, the same phenomenon of inexplicable knowledge applies to savants who calculate dates and calendars—instantly knowing dates and days throughout history.

Either way, the savant cannot explain why they are able to do what they do—a question I will dare to answer toward the end of our expedition. Incidentally, they can sometimes tell you *how*, (something of the method they use to discover the answer), as Tamment did with shapes and colors...but never *why* they, and not everyone, are able to do it. I will write more on this point shortly.

As we proceed you will also understand more of why I don't believe unseen forces are necessary to produce instant knowledge like Daniel's calculations, or Matt, and The Rain Man's, instant reading abilities as toddlers.

∼

Through a documentary on Rüdiger Gamm, another savant-level genius, I learned, all *true* savants can look at a display with random black dots and instantly tell how many dots it contains. The savant is shown an image of scattered dots and immediately says the number of dots e.g. "127." The Savant is nearly always correct. There doesn't seem to be enough time, (in our sense of time, which tics off in seconds) to count the dots. Our perception is correct, there isn't enough time to count them—the savant simply knows the answer. (Although, more complex calculations may take several seconds—suggesting some calculation.)

This phenomenon has to alter our understanding of time, because it has to be possible to calculate in fractions of a second (Remember the lightning fast neural network in our brain: *One million, million, million calculations a second? pg. 43*) Why couldn't it be possible for their brains to calculate lightning fast, then give them the number? After all, the power to do so is there. But, we can only *comfortably* imagine counting somewhere close to the speed at which we can speak the numbers. Gamm and Tamment's brain's obviously don't possess the same discomfort with counting faster than speech.

Adding more intrigue, Tamment is of a unique breed of mathematical savants who has what is called "*Synesthesia,*" which causes him to mentally see numbers as shapes and colors. This unusual aspect adds to the mystery of his type of ability, nudging it beyond our understanding of how mathematics exists in the world. When he sees the answer, he sees these colors and shapes representing the numbers—this is how he receives the answer.[3]

What if Tamment was consciously aware of the inner

---

[3] See un-conscious.com for videos on Daniel Tamment and Rüdiger Gamm

workings of his brain's calculating process, which is conducted using electrical signals that naturally emit colorful energy (sparks). So then, he sees the colors his neurons produce as his brain ignites to calculate specific numbers. If every time his brain accesses the number 6 for example, that neuron fires off as green in color, with a particular shape (remember, every neuron has its own shape). Tamment sees this function in his head (this is a question)? But, that doesn't answer all the questions. What do you think?

Daniel Tamment and Rüdiger Gamm are certainly permanent residents of The Zone.

This is a good place on our journey to take a break, and consider what we're seeing, before advancing.

ABSOLUTE KNOWLEDGE

Could this knowledge—to some extent—be innate?

What we do **know,** is that things like mathematics and physics are absolute facts—integral parts of our experience in the world (time and space). Mathematics is not something men have created, it is a *truth discovered*, observed, grasped with the eyes and mind, just like gravity and radio waves. Human beings have *discovered* knowledge of mathematics, physics, and such.

What I am getting at here is: I believe this knowledge is essential to our survival in this world, like knowledge of language, and therefore, comes **pre-installed on the hardware of our brains**—(but are, for some reason, difficult to fully grasp for most of us).

Dr. Darold A. Treffert speculates such in his book *Islands of Genius;* as he tries to understand how savants can *instantly* know things they have never learned. Dr. Treffert is referring to instantaneous knowledge. (Not what Tamment used to accurately recite the first 22,000 digits of pi. That was brain *memory*.) But, when Tamment instantly knew the square root of 135, or that June 12, 1810 was a Saturday, without looking at a calendar (I'm guessing) he demonstrated what appears to be unlearned knowledge. (The same with Matt Savage who acquired a mastery of the piano overnight.)

There was at least one scientific trial designed to cause normal people to acquire this instant counting ability. Although successful, it didn't come close to the savant's ability.[4] **However, the results did suggest this potential is latent in us all**, which supports my suspicion, hypothesis, and final conclusions. Sit tight though...we're getting there.

There are algorithms (step-by-step procedures), mathematicians use to quickly calculate dates and their corresponding day of the week, but savants haven't **learned** them—they simply **know**, and instantly use an algorithm[5]. It is possible (but not likely) they don't use an algorithm at all. (The idea of them knowing without any algorithm would be truly mystifying.) Rüdiger Gamm's closed eyes twitch while he is solving math problems. Indicating there are calculations going on—super fast calculations. In one test Rüdiger is said to—on the spot—**create** a previously unknown algorithm. Did he? Or did he just discover the *facts* related to the math puzzle?[6]

---

[4] http://www.centreforthemind.com/publications/SavantNumerosity.pdf
[5] I found one video on Youtube teaching this algorithm.
[6] http://un-conscious.com/videos/extraordinary-people-rudiger-gamm-part-1/

Absolute Innate Knowledge?

Consider this: Does a bird have to learn how to build a nest, or when and where to fly south? Does the ant need to learn how to forge tunnels and build the mound? The worker bee, to care for the Queen? The spider knows absolutely the technique and geometry of spinning the marvelous web...it is essential to its existence.

I share this to put Tamment's and others' ability in perspective. **What they do is not a something out of nothing "creative process;" but rather, a "discovery process." They tap into absolute (objective) knowledge.**

The Greek's called this knowledge of sight or perception *"oida"*: to become aware of the existence of a thing. And for a four year old to suddenly know (oida) reading can be quite a phenomenal thing, when all of his peers are blind to it.

Facts and truths are discovered by Daniel and Rüdiger much faster, and in a different way than they do for most people.

This is also true of musical and other savants. They will *hear* music and instantly recognize and understand its meaning and structure. If they have absolute pitch, they *instantly know* each sounds relationship to all sounds. Their knowledge in specific areas is truly transcendent—but not *otherworldly*. It is *relative*, thus connected with our natural human domain and its fundamental, necessary, aspects. Hence, Matt Savage could "solve the logic of the piano's 88 keys" overnight before age five.

I disagree with anyone who would say music is not essential to our existence (like language for example), but is purely creative. From my viewpoint, music could very well be categorized as "instinctive", because it is so universally connected to the souls of mankind, and is utilized as such.

Therefore, people like Tamment and Savage, through their ability to know things they have never learned or to quickly solve complex problems, tell us something about latent, fundamental human potential.

However, this remarkable ability is earthly, not otherworldly, even though few of us have access to its depths.

Experiential Knowledge

The knowledge we acquire through experience is variable (not fixed or absolute like the laws of math or music), because it comes through our interactions with people, things, or even principles. The Greeks distinguished this level of knowledge from *oida* and called it ***ginōskō***. This *experiential knowledge* is gained, and grows through our relationship with the subject. This knowledge has *progressed* from mere awareness and perception to experience.

You can see right away that this type of knowledge is nearly impossible for a human being who *instantly* knows facts related to a subject.

Experiential knowledge is subject to all kinds of influences. It's a product of our *understanding,* and the way we *interpret* our experiences. It is subjective (from my own point of view), and therefore may or not be true or factual for everyone else. On the other hand, absolute knowledge is assumed to be "objective fact," not affected by my individual interpretation.

The incredible abilities of the savants and prodigies we've studied do not come (because they know something no one else knows) from some unique personal experience—making the knowledge something new, original, or experiential. **He or she has merely *found* a way (or have been found by a way) to know some truth or fact without learning it beforehand.** I am by no means minimizing such phenomena. I am simply attempting to remove the tendency toward glorifying the individual.

So we have: absolute knowledge (Factual, awareness, or perception of the object)...Experiential knowledge (A more intimate knowledge and relationship with the subject).

Abstract Art

Let me illustrate how I see the difference between absolute and experiential knowledge, as it relates to human ability and performance.

Michael Angelo, the great artist who painted the ceiling of the Sistine Chapel in Rome, was a magnificent "draftsman." That is, he was able to capture real life, with a paint brush, in beautiful, picturesque form. This gift is comparable to *absolute knowledge*, it is factual—life as it is—for the most part.

Now, Picasso (also an exceptional draftsman), *became known* for his disfigured, abstract paintings. They were a distortion of reality, and represented to the art world a different perspective on reality. Picasso was able to take typical artistic expression, transform it in new ways—and for that he was applauded. As he aged his art became more and more an expression of his personal life and experiences. This is an example of what I am calling experiential knowledge. The artist is able to transfer his own unique feelings—based on perception and experience—into his medium (the canvas) for all to see.

The same observation can be made between regular/ rhythmic music, jazz fusion, and punk rock. Fusion and punk left behind the standard perception and principles of musical harmony, and "transformed" music. You may be able to think of other examples...dance, theatre, fashion, technology, etc.

Inspiration

Where does "*inspiration*" fit in the equation of transcendent performance, and the ability to transform an area of endeavor? Many of the aforementioned "great-ones" were inspired by other individuals, or by "chance encounters," which sparked a "stroke of genius," and subsequently led to their creative contributions to the world.

The fact that the spark which ignites extraordinary creativity doesn't come from within, doesn't minimize the *intimate knowledge* it takes to *make the connection* between the spark and its potential for transforming the subject. Add to this, the fact that most creative developments are triggered by some new knowledge, and *inspiration* has its place in the world of genius level creativity—in and out of The Zone region.

Why Most Savants and Prodigies Lack Experiential Knowledge

Remember in our discussion on Matt Savage (the child genius), I promised to re-visit the questions of whether or not a child genius is a permanent resident, and why most lack transcendence as adults?

Ellen Winner, in her book *Gifted Children* lists as "*Myth number 9*": the belief that "*gifted children become eminent adults.*" Her extensive research on a number of child prodigies and geniuses uncovered a sobering and unexpected reality:

> "Many gifted children, especially prodigies, burn out, while others move on to other areas of interest. Some, while extremely successful, never do anything genuinely creative."[7]

This popularly held "myth" is based on the seemingly logical idea that with exercise and use, any ability, knowledge, or endeavor, will grow exponentially. (Experience = more knowledge [ginōskō]= expertise—correct?) The reasoning goes something like this: "The person exercising the skill will become increasingly better at it, and ultimately reach a level where he or she can improve (creativity) on the world's knowledge in that area. Certainly, if the *child* has an *adult mastery* of the skill, he has a head start, and is destined to out-perform the adults he is currently equal to, and leave his peers far behind."

Ellen Winner accepts the theory that it takes at least 10 years of hard work in an area to reach a level of competence necessary to "transform your domain" through some original creativity. This explains, somewhat, why child prodigies don't transcend in their area of talent: not enough development.

I believe there may be yet another (similar) explanation as to why most child prodigies or savants—for that matter—do not become eminent adults who transform their area of expertise. They lack the experiential knowledge needed to truly know a thing intimately enough to transform or reshape it. My explanation appears to repeat that of Ellen Winner, but it is slightly different, because it begins *without* the expectation

---

[7] *Gifted Children*, Ellen Winner, 1996 pg 312

of the child genius becoming exponentially greater as he matures. **Spending time with someone or something doesn't automatically guarantee you will acquire *intimate* knowledge.**

A child, in theory, can only possess *absolute knowledge* of a subject, because of inexperience. Child prodigies, geniuses, and savants have an abundance of the objective knowledge. A blessing on one hand, and a possible curse at the same time, if that which is lacking (namely, experience, and maturity) is ignored or overlooked in their caretaker's mad dash to the bank and the unstable pedestal of fame. It appears, the earlier the genius is discovered and celebrated, the less likely the genius is to blossom to full expectations—he/she has already arrived.

A Gift

I want to add here yet another factor contributing to prodigies' lack of transcendence as adults: **I believe true creativity to be a gift. It is a distinct talent in the same way that genius itself is.** This is one reason why very few geniuses demonstrate transformative creativity: they lack the gift of creativity.

Knowing all the "facts" related to a subject is quite a bit different from knowing a thing inside-out, upside-down, and from many conceivable and *inconceivable* angles. The former is impressive, but the latter makes it possible to connect your subject with everything it is minutely related to, because you see/understand more of its parts. When a related object or idea appears, the creatively *gifted one* is able to make the association with the subject, because she knows her subject intimately. She is then able to transform the world's appreciation by broadening their knowledge of the subject. This explains the difference between oida (knowledge/perception) and ginōskō (knowledge turned intimate).

Question: Can a "gifted" child prodigy possess this kind of knowledge? According to Ellen Winner's research, very few— if any—do.

I would imagine it is a sobering thing to realize the extraordinary child is not a "little man" or "little woman," equipped to perform as adults, but is, in fact, an immature child who happens to have adult level specific knowledge.

It is also likely that child prodigies—like other genius' on a savant level—are **conditioned by very strong networks in a particular area**—to resist change. There often appears to be an "obsession" in whatever area of talent they have, which would distract them from developing and maturing through broader experiential knowledge. Unfortunately, our world requires so many areas of competence: social, emotional, etc., which the child denied the opportunity to mature through experience in these areas will be handicapped as an adult, as the lives of too many early bloomers have proven.

(We will expand on these ideas in chapter 10.)

The phenomenal performance of child prodigies, geniuses, and savants is impressive all the same, and force us to consider what resides (latent) in all of us.

Let's continue our exploration of permanent Zone residents and raise our level of amazement before we leave this area:

The Human Camera

The Eye, The Hand, The Memories: My own artistic ability, on the scale of brain power and human potential, is well above the norm, somewhere around a fast moving stream. A savant like Stephen Wiltshire,[8] also known as *"The Human Camera,"* is a waterfall of artistic ability. He's the epitome of human potential in art (drawing, sketching). In fact, I still cannot fully grasp the reality of what he does—it stretches my belief in what is humanly possible.

We should note, Wiltshire's incredible genius level knowledge is of the objective, absolute type, not the experiential type. Let's ponder just how incredible Stephen's ability is.

He was taken up by helicopter to view the city of Rome for 45 minutes, and then asked to draw the city from memory. Wow, I just noticed this sounds a lot like "The Rain Man's" gift—who could recite the details of any book he had ever read. He knew history like an encyclopedia—if he read it he remembered it.

After three days, and five and a half yards of paper (hung in a curved rectangular, panoramic shape), he completed the drawing task without a second view of the city. You will want to view the link to the youtube video I have referenced, it is fascinating.

Let me give a summary, and draw some conclusions (as I see them) regarding his ability. Wiltshire's drawing was incredibly, transcendently accurate. For that to be possible, he has to possess a pure photographic memory. That is to say, his brain has to record and retrieve an exact picture of what his eyes saw one day...two days...and three days before—like a perfect file on a hard drive. This is—if we had not witnessed it with our own eyes—impossible to comprehend on planet earth. It is beyond what we know to be humanly possible.

---

[8] http://goo.gl/gGLeq

Even recent memories fade—we know this from experience. (This begs us to extract some meaning.)

Insight From Magic

You know, magicians make a living from the scientifically proven phenomenon of "selective human observation." Humans just don't see everything in front of them, and if asked to recollect a scene, they will miss 95% of the details. This is a puzzling, but true, phenomenon—eye witness testimony is woefully unreliable.

I recently experienced this phenomenon after witnessing a traffic accident. After talking for at least 20 minutes with one of the people involved in the accident, I was asked to give a statement to a police officer. I could not remember what color clothing the guy (now gone) was wearing. I was unsure whether he was wearing pants or shorts. I had looked this guy in the face for 20 minutes or more, touched his shoulder, noticed some wounds, but drew fuzzy images when it came to positive recollection. Like Stephen, I too am an artist. Go figure, this incident shook my faith in my own sense of sight.

Back to Wiltshire's remarkable, astounding artistic feat!

We are not talking about one object, or a few objects, but hundreds of thousands, probably millions of objects, lines, and shapes—an entire city neighborhood! Remember, realistic art is based on the proper intersecting of lines and shapes, so each stroke has to have the correct meaning for the final picture to be true.

One of the things that stood out to me while viewing his drawing was the vehicles he placed on the streets. They were in very good perspective. This is an area which I struggle with as an artist, because it is very difficult to draw an object at the proper angle from your viewing perspective—even if you are looking directly at it. This skill requires either:

A. A photographic memory, along with the ability to transfer the exact image from your head, through to your hands and onto the paper; all the while the picture in your heads is never lost, because you are literally projecting it onto the paper, and tracing it with your hands.

B. The picture is copied intermittently, as your eyes move back and forth between your mind and the paper as you draw. The picture is retrieved intermittently, as interruptions occur over the 3 day period.

If the picture in your head is lost or fuzzy, you will have to rely on knowledge and experience; this is where many good artists like myself fail, and have to refer to models, photos, or some other reference for accuracy.

Wiltshire drew everything, including those vehicles on the roads from his helicopter's viewpoint, exactly in the perspective he saw them. His final work was even overlaid by a photograph, and was unbelievably accurate.

Perspective requires some understanding of the geometrical relationship between objects and their relationship to the horizon and your viewpoint. As an autistic savant, Wiltshire hasn't studied the theory of perspective, but has an innate knowledge (oida) of what—for most—is a complex science to be learned through study.

It is very possible that Wiltshire's brain and *"The Rain Man's"* brain have strengths in the same exact areas relating to photographic memory. The difference between them, being their areas of specialization, interest, and talent. The "Rain Man" (Kim Peak) recalls written information with photographic clarity, while the "Human Camera" recalls visual images with the same clarity. Perhaps the "Rain Man" saw information in books as images also.

When I have to recall information from a book, I will usually remember where on the page I originally read it. So I see the information, and the place I read it at the same time. Stephen and Kim Peak would recall the entire book of information—every bit—including page numbers.

Stephen's abilities are no doubt examples of our brains "potential" in the area of memory, storage, retrieval, and mastery of an area of interest. But the question arises, for which scientists are searching for an answer: Is this ability available for everyone to tap into? We are on our way to offering an answer to that question as we move through this book, but for now, I present to you one more permanent **citizen** of The Zone of extraordinary performance.

Transcendent Sensual Power

Ben Underwood was a teenager who lived in Sacramento, California. He lost his eyesight at the age of two. Sometime soon after losing his sight, he developed a sense of the presence of objects around him by hearing sound waves bounce off of them. For example, while riding in a car, he could tell that an object was a skyscraper.

Shortly thereafter he developed the ability to generate sound waves by making clicking sounds with his mouth—exactly like bats, dolphins, and submarine sonar.[9] The clicking ability created more detailed pictures of objects, because he was now able to generate his own targeted sound waves to bounce off them. He used this ability as *echo location* to navigate his way around objects with the near precision of eyesight. Video shows him rollerblading in and out of cars on his street...playing basketball with his friends...among other unlikely activities for a blind person.

Remember my introduction's comparison of TZP in significance to natural disasters like tornados? **Think about what these permanent residents of The Zone were/are able to accomplish, and try to tell yourself that it doesn't mean anything about human potential on planet earth.**

This echo location ability enabled Underwood to live an incredibly mobile life, interacting more fully with the world around him. If anything, he added a new perspective for nonscientists on the presence, power, and usefulness of sound waves all around us. (We are moving closer to a meaning of these phenomena.)

Once he acquired this ability, he kept it until his untimely death. Ben received permanent residence into The Zone of maximized human potential.

Later we'll discuss more about Underwood, analyze his ability, and what it means for us "normal" human beings.

If these residents represent our true potential, what should be our personal expectations? Should we settle for common mediocrity? (There can certainly be complacency, even comfort, in the crowd.)

---

[9] http://un-conscious.com/videoscategory/unconscious-videos/

CHAPTER FIVE

The Road To The Zone

"The road to the Zone is paved with NEED.
—jw

Before we examine more of The Zone's amazing power, let's find the roads that lead there. How does one get there? Until now, we have only been able to hear of its power, and observe its influence from a distance; like a spectator in the valley, needing binoculars to observe a distant city on a mountaintop (or as some have described it, a mysterious island). We need to move closer.

I have used two main sources of information in my investigative work, to ascertain the exact path or paths leading to The Zone.

The most reliable sources were:

- The testimony of The Zone's residents as to how they gained access to The Zone.

- Observation: Any good investigator has to be a keen observer; able to gather the details, read between the lines, and draw conclusions, which may not be clearly expressed or obvious to the undiscerning eye and ear.

Unfortunately, we are not able to find anyone to interview

who is on their way to The Zone. Therefore, the only way for us to determine which road was taken to reach that state, is to look back at the circumstances which lead up to the phenomenon. Hence, our two sources of investigation.

Two Roads

From my investigations, I discovered there are two roads (ways of access) to The Zone; one is mostly **voluntary**; which suggests deliberate conscious input. The other is completely **involuntary**. The one involves—to some extent—an act of the will, the other is purely unconscious. Let's look at the second road first, because it is the most common road taken.

INVOLUNTARY ACCESS ROAD

From the man who knows complex facts and skills he never learned...to the gifted musician who claims inspiration for a mesmerizing composition...to the professional athlete who out performs herself to set a world record...to the man who taps into every ounce of power in his body to do the improbable...to the professional athlete who outperforms all of his peers during a record breaking trek...to the average Joe who—out of the blue—shaves 15 strokes off his golf score, there runs the distinctive thread of *involuntary privilege*.

   No amount of scientific theory can erase the candid observation that The Zone is predominately an involuntary phenomenon. Hence, it is essentially an UN-CONSCIOUS state.

   With any attempt to unlock the mysteries of transcendent human performance, we must not deny the reality of *involun-*

tary inspiration: or escalation of individual potential. A failure to notice, or a decision to ignore this most glaring characteristic of human transcendence, is to begin the journey of discovery on the wrong path. On the other hand, to recognize the overwhelming presence of the involuntary aspect of this phenomenon is to approach the phenomenon face to face.

Gate Keeper of The Zone

The brain is our supervisor of all reality, which we receive through our senses. Because The Zone is mostly a *brain-initiated state*—the person is initially passive, and experiences a sensation similar to a trance, hypnosis, or daydreaming. (We saw this clearly in chapter two's temporary residents and chapter three's lengthy discussion on the brain.).

We found: If the subject is aware of what is happening, he/she cannot explain it adequately with words—the *understanding* appears to be impaired. Therefore, they are likely to attribute the phenomenon to the wrong cause. Savants and genius', who are permanent residents of The Zone, are unable to explain how they came about their extraordinary gifts. They may or may not be able to explain how their extraordinary ability works—but as to "why," they are clueless.

The answer as to why, resides in what I call "involuntary privilege"—a gift: *beneficium*.

This puzzle is observed when an athlete has trouble explaining to reporters the cause of the exceptional performance they just demonstrated. Players will say something like "I was just feeling it," "I was hot," etc. They are essentially saying, "I was swept into The Zone...I didn't expect it...It was mostly involuntary, and I let it flow."

On the other hand, their coaches (who, of course, are paid to explain the causes of such a performance and hopefully help repeat it), will offer a plausible explanation based on something tangible, like training, or mind-set, that produced the performance. In essence, they're saying the cause was *voluntary,* and therefore consciously *repeatable.* More on this shortly.

The main reason the person is unable to explain how or why they experienced this phenomenon, is they are not aware of doing anything to cause it. They don't know the cause—but remember the feelings.

All roads that lead to The Zone of transcendence have a degree of involuntariness to them; although, there is one road that is nearly 100 percent involuntary. This road is the path traveled by the permanent citizens—born into The Zone— like savants and geniuses. Those individuals who become permanent citizens later in life, such as acquired savants (like Rüdiger Gamm and Jason Pagett), have been granted access by means of the same involuntary road. These residents have clearly reached that region through no effort of their own. Many, in fact, have been *born* with evidence of The Zone's power already on them.

Whereas, most other residents, such as automobile lifters and other temporary residents, have arrived from a path that may be explained by natural "voluntary" influences.

VOLUNTARY ACCESS ROAD

The second road of access to The Zone, which I call *voluntary,* is triggered by some conscious event, such as an emergency. The person is fully conscious, and because the situation demands super human performance, *the brain initiates* and grants access to The Zone state.

You will remember the report I shared of Lauren Kornacki, the 22-year old woman who lifted a 2,000 pound car off of her dad and saved his life. A few weeks later, Carlos Castro lifted an SUV to save his friend's life. Both are examples of voluntary access into The Zone region.

(You may already be making the connection with "fight or flight, adrenal response"— we'll discuss that soon.)

⁓

As I was pondering these and similar examples of car lifting to save the lives of loved ones: I began to wonder why we don't hear of the man trapped under the car receiving super human strength to free himself. Then I was reminded of the following incident that caught my attention and imagination at the beginning of my research on this phenomenon. This incident flips the pattern.

This real life story highlights the extraordinary ability of our brain to take over in an emergency situation, and maximize the potential of every part of our body, to get us out of a situation that would destroy a mere mortal, and provide temporary access to the extraordinary resources of The Zone.

This is a case of the man under the fallen car freeing himself.

In 1999, Sinjin Eberle suddenly became super strong when he was almost killed under a thousand pound slab of mountain.[1] He needed to quickly figure a way to save his own life, and received super human strength in response to his need to survive.

---

[1] http://un-conscious.com/videos/achieving-super-human-strength-24/

While climbing with a friend, Eberle reached for a part of the mountain to support and pull himself up, when the entire side of the mountain came loose and landed on top of him. Pinned under the half ton slab of mountain, (the impact should have knocked him unconscious.)...flat on his back, sliding down the incline of the mountain toward the edge of the cliff...it took everything within him to keep from being crushed. His friend (and climbing partner) was only able to see his shoes sticking out from under the giant slab. Just before going over the cliff, he pushed that huge slab of mountain off of himself and over the mountain side.

Experts said: to accomplish that feat, his *brain triggered* his chest, arms, and shoulder muscles to exert every bit of strength in them. They say he used 80 percent more muscle power than any man ever uses under normal strenuous physical activity. The exertion was so powerful that he damaged his upper body in the process of surviving.

This gives us insight into the kind of muscle power it took to lift those cars—but this time from the perspective of the one being crushed!

That incident and similar ones, illustrate "voluntary access" into The Zone—where a person **needs to perform,** and the brain delivers much more than expected. Maximum power is only released by our brain when it detects a dire emergency, or it has **unexpectedly taken total control to induce** The Zone Phenomenon.

This is a key finding in my investigation of this phenomenon.

The brain is the governor; It holds the key to unlocking the gate into that territory of transcendence. The subject (person) for which it is responsible, is by all accounts passive, or involuntarily carried along into The Zone of super human performance.

There is a *voluntary request*—a *need* from the conscious mind that triggers the brain into action. Contrast this with the unexplainable *involuntary* Zone experiences which have **no discernible cause.**

CHAPTER SIX

Keys To The City

"Where there's a will there's a pathway"
—jw

While we are unable to influence a purely *"involuntary"* entry into The Zone (such as child prodigies, savants, and other geniuses experience); the *"voluntary"* road to access is paved with input received from the would-be resident of The Zone. The athlete who surges past her competitors...the rock climber who needs power to save his life...the music composer under inspiration...all have, in some way *induced* The Zone Phenomenon.

It is these voluntary triggers and keys, which initiate access to The Zone, and open the gate to the phenomenon, that I want us to consider. "If I can do something to cause this phenomenon, I want to know what it is!"

If indeed, the brain controls this phenomenon, we have to make sure we understand how it does so, in order to cooperate with it. If the brain initiates the plan, and navigates the journey, we just need to be available for the expedition; or know how to request a ticket.

Our Brain: Proven Proficiency—Capable Pilot

From the moment of conception, when the sperm and egg come together as a single cell, begin to divide and divide and divide—ultimately resulting in this conglomeration of the trillions of cells we call a human body—our brain begins to manage the complex processes and tasks involved in the operation of the body.

Around 4 weeks after conception your nervous system began to take shape including your brain. By the end of the next 8 weeks (week 12 of fertilization), your brain is completely formed[1]. By week 20 your brain is managing input from the senses, and you can hear and distinguish your mother's voice. Remember 250,000 neurons per minute are being formed.

After birth, we know one of the brain's primary objectives is to accomplish all processes and tasks in the easiest way possible. It desires the most direct, efficient pathway to performing and accomplishing all processes and tasks; to the extent that most of the body's processes and tasks are *automatic*—we don't have to *think* about them. (We will see later why it is important to remember this primary objective of the brain.)

There is a distinction between what our brains accomplish through primary innate programming in our DNA, and what our brains accomplish through learning and adapting. The proficiency of our brains in the primary, "pre-programmed" functions and tasks, lets us know its *potential* to accomplish what it is *designed* to do in the other—conscious—areas, involving learning, performing and adapting. If it has proven capable in the big things like nervous system function, physi-

---

[1] http://www.baby2see.com/development/first_trimester.html

cal and sensory development, why should I doubt its ability in the smaller things?

This fact is profound if we think about it. We so innately understand and believe this, that we trust our brains to re-member what's important, and manage our development in this world. We don't carry a life-long note pad with things like "look both ways before you cross the street," "don't touch fire," "put one foot in front of the other," "chew meat thoroughly," "beware of the guy in the ski mask," etc. We trust the brain to remember.

We are inclined to take for granted the brain's ability to perfectly perform the tasks needed for life...until of course, something goes wrong due to some kind of brain injury. Then, we find we may need to re-learn tasks we never had to think about before. (Don't forget it's a privilege.)

It is the second area of the brain's responsibilities that we are often confused about: its capability to accomplish learning and adapting tasks (which are always changing), with the same precision, proficiency, and ease, by which it ac-complishes the "automatic" tasks and processes. This is where I want to linger for a while.

Your Brain and the Need to Learn, Adapt

The subtitle of this section is *"where there is a will there is a pathway,"* because all of the brain's tremendous accomplish-ments appear to be based on what is *necessary,* or what the body or person *needs.* All of the processes that originate in our DNA, such as growth, breathing, and physical mobility, are necessary for life. They are imperative. They *must* be ac-complished. I know that we can survive without the ability to perform some tasks, but we are talking about the ideal—all systems are working perfectly—scenario. The main focus here is *"need,"* and how our brain responds to what our bodies need to accomplish.

When it comes to learning and adapting there is no difference. Our brain will attempt to learn the most efficient and easy way to accomplish whatever task our body is in the process of learning. If we are asking our brain to learn something, it takes for granted some level of need, and therefore, responds accordingly.

I am amazed at the details I remember from my childhood. It never fails that when I remember something from decades ago, it was very important at the time it occurred. My brain stored that information as important for easy retrieval. I remember an incident when I was in preschool, and was concerned that my younger sister not be embarrassed. My parents made a big deal about this because of my age...it surprised them. I remember this event because it shaped my self-image, and the way I would understand the impact and importance of my own personal values on those around me. I had no idea at the age of five, that I would never forget this event; but my brain decided it was significant, so I've never forgotten.

Unfortunately, or fortunately (depending on how you look at it), the brain will stamp like a hot iron any threatening situation as a defense measure for future protection. All you have to do is recall some of your earlier memories, like a neighborhood or school yard bully.

So we can see that the brain itself prioritizes according to needs or level of importance when it comes to memory. This is an automatic brain function.

Now, the question still remains: is the brain capable of learning and forging the pathway to accomplishing new tasks, with the same level of incredible proficiency it does with the other "important for sustaining life" stuff, like breathing and immune function? We know that we only have to learn to walk once, ride a bike once, swim once, etc. So the answer to that question should be *yes*. The brain has proven by empirical evidence that it is *more than capable*.

So then, this should give us **confidence** in the brain's ability to lead us into The Zone region of maximum potential.

How Your Brain Responds to Need:

The Discovery Channel recorded a documentary titled *The Miraculous Mind*. One particular segment discusses the brain's ability to recover from damage caused by trauma. The segment follows a Japanese man who documented the collapse and recovery of his wife after a stroke. Her heart stopped for a few minutes, and she was almost brain dead. She was in a coma for nearly two months. The illness set this late middle aged woman back to an apparent infantile mentality, with very poor motor functions. She also lost the ability to walk or care for herself. The film opens with her reaching a milestone: learning to count again.

Much of the left side of her brain was destroyed due to the loss of blood flow that causes a stroke. Brain cells die rapidly when blood flow is cut off, and remember, they will never re-generate.

This documentary (which you can view on my blog[2]) points out that a stroke destroys the brain's system of commu-

---
[2] http://alturl.com/6rsoi

nication networks between neurons. Each neuron communicates with other neurons through chemical messages sent through bursts of electrical charges. If the neurons that control walking are destroyed or can't communicate, then your ability to walk will be affected.

What we learn from the woman in this documentary, and similar victims' recovery, is that the brain is magnificently resilient. Scientists call this phenomenon "plasticity." Remaining healthy neurons can step in and take over the functions and responsibilities of dead or damaged neurons, forging new pathways to accomplish the desired tasks. Remaining healthy neurons respond to the **need** to recover functions and abilities lost through something like a stroke.

The video is very enlightening and powerful, because it shows the axon's (tentacles, see diagram pg. 29) of a healthy neuron reaching out, growing as it seeks to connect with other neurons, and establish connections around a damaged area. This is fascinating, and is impossible to see with the human eye without with the aid of super powerful microscopes.

A Pattern For All Needs

I can only assume that this is the way the brain initially establishes all of the networks and pathways necessary for us to function in the world. Those 250,000 neurons are being formed every minute, over the nine months gestation period. This video also helps us picture those neurons reaching out to each other, as that little toddler begins to grow and *interact with the world around him*, establishing networks, forging pathways, and accomplishing tasks.

The involuntary/unconscious nature of this aspect of the

brain's function in response to a need is a significant part of what that I propose in this book. I will share more implications and insights from this brain documentary a little later, but for now more on the dynamics of need.

Need/Request for Access: Adrenaline

Adrenaline (epinephrine) is one of those chemical messengers of communication used in our brain and nervous system. Some of us are familiar with the process of our body producing adrenaline in emergency situations, in what is called *"fight or flight response."* Also known as the "get the heck out of here, or fight for your life!" response. Well, adrenaline is released by a *conscious* need for help. I guess we can think of it—in terms of The Zone—as a request from normal life for access to The Zone region of extraordinary performance—albeit emergency access! I'll share more facts about adrenaline a little later.

THE POWER OF NEED

I have a theory derived from a couple decades of fascination with the world's sports obsession, and the peculiar characteristics of top performing, dominant, athletes who fuel that obsession.

Much has been said (in the area of self help) about the power of positive thinking, and its effect on one's ability to achieve. But, to my knowledge, not much has been offered to show why this is the case, other than the stories of some who attribute their fame and success to positive thinking.

I'd like to take this theory a little further, and offer a more concrete reason why the theory of positive mental attitude is on the right track…essential for success…and therefore indispensable as one seeks keys to TZP of transcendence.

Formulating a theory about a common link between the mental or psychological characteristics of dominant athletes and top performers is not an easy thing. When asked for an explanation, many who are able, (sometimes it's hard to define with words), and willing, (some might want to keep trade secrets), to express the inner workings of their mind as it contributes to their success, credit hard work, strong desire, practice, and similar things.

Strong Desire

I want to focus on the common **"strong desire"** that all dominant performers share, and hopefully suggest a deeper insight into what and why this attribute is *critical* for "voluntary" access into The Zone; which top athletes and performers experience more often than the rest.

Strong desire is a type of positive thinking; although it goes beyond thoughts, and reaches the will and determination of top performers.

One of the reasons this hypothesis is difficult to prove, is because nearly **all** competitive athletes and individuals possess the same "strong desire to win and succeed"—especially at the professional level. I doubt anyone reaches the top of their profession without a strong desire to succeed.

So, how can this be a key ingredient on the road to The Zone, if nearly all top performers possess it? Perhaps it's better to ask: why do a few excel above the rest if they all possess the same desire, and relatively the same level of skill, training, expertise, and hatred for losing?

I just mentioned that a strong desire/need is a key ingredient in the mix on the road to The Zone. **It is a fact that top competitors possess this key factor in varying degrees and quality.** When I say quality I mean *purity*, like pure gold, as opposed to a contaminated mineral, that hasn't been forged with fire to removed impurities. *Many experts and analysts overlook this distinction when they compare greatness.* Let's not make that mistake—***need* varies in quality or purity.**

Need vs. Want: Forging New Pathways

I mentioned the Discovery Channel documentary[3] on the brain, which includes fascinating up close footage of brain neurons establishing connections between themselves. The big picture of what the brain does is this: the 100 billion or so neurons we are born with begin to communicate as soon as the brain is formed in the womb, and it becomes responsible for maintaining and managing the life functions which the DNA doesn't directly handle; It appears a large part of its responsibility is managing interactions with the world. In other words, the brain assumes its role in our development as soon as genetics or DNA determine. It is possible—as far as I know—that the first two brain cells communicate some information between themselves. It is safe to say that when the time is right, the brain assumes its enormous role of master manager and regulator of the conscious human being.

A newborn baby's brain has already made approximately 17% of the *trillions* of connections between the 100 billion

---

[3] http://alturl.com/6rsoi ; The Brain Our Universe Within: The Miraculous Mind (Discovery Channel): Confused signals sent (29 min. mark of video)

neurons. Remember, each neuron can connect with thousands of other neurons. As more connections, or *pathways* are formed, the newborn begins to accomplish learning and development. Next time you look at that little bitty baby, think of the work that brain is doing.

As the newborn begins to interact with the world around him the brain begins to analyze, interpret, and utilize the information that is being received and to make the appropriate connections between neurons, so that the child develops and interacts in an efficient, capable, and beneficial way with the world around him.

Most of what is learned and established through early development becomes hard-wired in solid networks between billions of neurons, and will *never* have to be relearned. In fact, it will become *very difficult* to undo what is learned in the early years. *This is why I emphasize that the brain strives to make everything we learn as EASY as possible. This is its obvious genetically ingrained purpose.* This is a very important point if we are trying to understand The Zone Phenomenon, because its helps us let go and trust the brain to do what it is designed to do—and is capable of doing.

The Lesson from Damaged Neurons

The documentary I'm referring to demonstrates what happens when neurons are damaged, and a connection between neurons is broken. This is very interesting, and offers deeper insight into our discussion on "***need.***"

When a neuron is damaged—as in the case of a traumatic brain injury—many of the healthy neurons in the area begin to reach out to form new connections around the damaged area, in an attempt to pick up the slack left by the damaged neuron. During this process the person who suffered the injury is experiencing recovery or re-habilitation. As effective, new connections are established, the individual will reap the benefits, and experience a fuller recovery.

During the process of recovery, many neurons that tried to help by reaching out for new connections die off as they are not needed. The brain attempts to create the best connections, which will result in fully recovering the same ability that was lost. When, and if this is accomplished, unneeded connections are allowed to die off, and the stronger ones remain. (This same phenomenon occurs naturally with age: as we get older we loss unnecessary neural connections.)

The purpose of physical therapy or any rehabilitation is to teach **one way—the optimal way—**for the individual to perform a task, so that the proper neurons will establish and maintain connections. **The result of successful therapy will be the fullest recovery possible, with the task or function performed as close to easy and automatic as possible.**

In the case of a need to re-learn walking, physical therapy creates the **need**, from which the brain gets its directions as to which pathways to establish. *That need is hammered in by the repetition of therapy.*

We are now beginning to see where "positive thinking" comes in. The repetition of thoughts, desire, and will, can, may, and will become needs, thereby establishing powerful pathways to accomplishment.

Where There's a Will...

The marvelous thing (in every sense of the word), is that if I become unable to walk because of a brain injury, physical therapy will instruct my brain *how* to produce steps, and my brain will find a way to make it happen. This happens every day, all over the world. It is marvelous!

In the same way, if I determine to learn a new language, give my brain the directive/command, and begin instructions, my brain will not only make it happen, but eventually make it as *easy and automatic* as possible. *Understanding this natural process will equip you with the **patience and unwavering will** it takes to allow this process to work to completion.* If I determine to acquire a new skill, my brain is capable of making that happen.

This is where the ***will, command, demand, or need*** come in.

Needs and Wants and Priorities

Again, as we consider the ability of the brain to manage and forge the networks between neurons, which produce all of the tasks and functions we perform as human beings; we have to distinguish between what we direct the brain to do (i.e. will or desire), and what it does automatically as a result of genetic programming.

For the purpose of our discussion on finding keys to The Zone, we will focus most of our attention on what we consciously or unconsciously ***direct*** our brain to do, and how it responds.

In the performance of sports the needs are dynamic, always changing. The genetic functions that the brain controls such as breathing, physical maturity, regulating hormones, heartbeat, body temperature, immunity, etc., are critical to our survival, and are not left to our conscious control (thank God!). We are subject to error and indecision—we'd forget to breathe if it were in our conscious control!

This fact of life gives insight into how the brain handles and processes the less critical information and directives it receives during something like sports competition.

It is reasonable to conclude that the brain prioritizes according to NEED. That is, the most critical tasks and functions are given top priority, much like physical therapy. In this scenario, directives or commands to the brain, based on what we want but don't need, will receive less priority. In other words the brain is programmed to distinguish between what is critical and what can wait.

This is very similar to the way our body's liver (the cleansing and chemical processing filter) is designed to function. For example: experts say (alcohol triggered) cirrhosis of the liver happens because, when alcohol is ingested in large quantity it is given top priority, due to its potential danger to the body. The alcoholic person continues to consume high volumes of alcohol, and as a result the liver is taxed with trying to clean and filter what has become toxic, and neglects other needed functions. It finally loses the fight.

In the same way, the brain prioritizes according to the needs placed upon it. The more critical the need, the more responsibility, control, and urgency, the brain assumes to meet that need. If the brain controls The Zone experience we can see the problem here: it may be handling other priorities when you want access to The Zone.

Even in an ***involuntary*** Zone experience where the performer is *swept* into this state, the principle of NEED is present. How do I know this? **Everyone who has experienced The Zone unexpectedly has testified to "not having anything else on their mind", they were in a pleasant, sleep walking type of state. There were no demands on their minds other than the task at hand.** The **need** was induced by the brain, and the **goal** was proficient performance of the task at hand.

When Needs Collide In The Zone!

The power of need plays a pivotal role when opposing competitors are both invited into The Zone. The need to win imposed by the will, and taken up as a duty by the brain, initiates entrance into The Zone. The body is merely a vehicle at the disposal of the brain, commandeered to accomplish its mission.

Well, surprisingly enough, don't expect a lot of scoring because defensive performance is as incredible as offensive output when competitors meet in The Zone.

Case in point is the longest tennis match in history[4] mentioned earlier (pg. 24). **The immovable object meets the irresistible force!** Both players played incredible offense and defense, literally neutralizing each other, to a seemingly endless and exhausting standoff. I didn't watch it, but was glued to every bit of the news coverage that followed. It was amazing to see and contemplate.

---

[4] Copyright 2010 by The Associated Press http://sports.espn.go.com/ sports/tennis/wimbledon10/news/story?id=5322284

John Isner of the United States finally defeated Nicolas Mahut of France, after a match that lasted more than eleven hours, over three days. The score in the fifth set was 70-68, with a total of 138 games.

This was a Zone competition if there ever was one, and both competitors were swept into it that fateful week.

The eventual winner, Isner, allowed only one service break in the entire final set. "I wasn't really thinking," Isner said. "We played the greatest match ever, in the greatest place to play tennis," Mahut said, who was ranked 148th. "I thought he would make a mistake. I waited for that moment, and it never came."

"I'm tired watching this," joked John McEnroe (past Wimbledon champion). "It's Herculean what they're doing...I had to come pay my respects."

"It was the will to win. Not that I out-willed him; I mean, obviously, he gave it his all," Isner said. "I just kind of was a little bit more fortunate than he was."

They were both fortunate to experience that type of phenomenon at the same time, **and need expressed by will was the driving force.**

∿

When Tiger Woods finally won a tournament in March 2012—after a 2 ½ year draught—he was asked in the post tournament press conference something to the effect of: "Do you feel the need to win?" Tiger's response—as though he has heard that question before—was: "The need idea is false—"I *want* to win," he explained; as though need suggests weakness. (Remember my distinction on "quality" of needs among top performers? They all have need, but quality/degree vary.)

Question: **Is it possible for someone to need something and not be consciously aware of it?** Of course, it happens all the time. As a matter of fact, most needs are handled automatically by the body, without deliberate conscious awareness by the person. Do you need toxic waste disposal? Your body takes care of that. Do you need to enter puberty? Your body takes care of that. The author of the book *The Water Cure* says: in his experience, most adults are not aware that they are dehydrated, and as a result, they don't drink enough water to prevent the many diseases caused by dehydration. They are consciously unaware of the desperate need of their body's cells. The need is latent, yet very real. How many lovers fail to realize their NEED for their partner until they're gone, then despair and instability sets in.

So, was Tiger lying when he said he didn't *need* to win, but merely *wants* to win? No, because he may not necessarily be conscious of the fact that the level of his want had reached that of a need. Or, that his want to win was fueled by a *deeper* need.

In my opinion, he desires to win, and is driven by this need in an unusually powerful way. His statements throughout his career confirm a level of need that has disregard (or contempt) for any barrier threatening to keep him from satisfying that need.

It is a fact, that many—if not all—of the highest performers in sports and the business world, possess an overwhelming need to win, or be the best. They often exhibit a type of merciless contempt for their opponents (and sometimes the rules), with a dog eat dog/survival of the fittest mentality. Think of Bill Gates, Steve Jobs, Sir Richard Branson and many others—reports say. There is simply a **need** to overcome any obstacle that would prevent success.

By contrast, every other top performer wants to win. Or has a strong desire to win, but it's not absolutely critical—they can live with less. If you could look into their hearts, you will find the *strongest* need elsewhere. This is not a fault; it's simply a distinguishing characteristic among those at the top.

I'm not sure exactly how much "the great one's" exceptional skills and gifts *drive them* to realize their full potential, or how much *the raw need to feed* on trophies drives them to achieve greater heights through learning, training, maturing, and succeeding.

Another key: Tiger Woods confessed to literally "hating to lose", and "expected to win" every tournament he played in. Many other exceptional athletes say, "I hope to win." In business, the tycoon: Sir Richard Branson exhibited this same attitude and resolve in many bold, interesting, and successful ways.

I suspect this deep need to win began at a very early age, and was accompanied by a drive to learn, practice, and discipline themselves. It is reinforced as a result of increased skill, ability, and success, and will only diminish with age or as the "need to feed" diminishes.

Make no mistake. Need is a driving force and KEY prerequisite for the brain to open the pathways of voluntary access into The Zone Phenomenon.

Gifts, Talents, and Delusions

Exceptional talent will enable an athlete to consistently excel in his sport, but The Zone is a different level of performance. It is indeed a distinct territory above the realm of talent and skill.

An illustration of this point (i.e. delusions), comes to mind when I think of a talented athlete running into an opponent performing in The Zone: The ferocious Mike Tyson against Buster Douglas, heavyweight boxing match. Buster Douglas fought on a level which neither he—or "Iron" Mike Tyson for that matter—had ever seen, or would ever see again.

Tyson was a punisher...rock hard...seasoned heavyweight champ, who (on paper) never should have lost to Buster Douglas. But, when The Zone is present it doesn't matter who the opponent is, because a brain operating in The Zone will not allow many, if any, mistakes.

Buster not only stood toe to toe with Tyson, and took his bruising punches, but gained confidence as the fight progressed. He put on a clinic of offensive and defensive boxing strategy and execution. You would've thought he was the champ, and Tyson was a sparring partner.

Some will say Tyson was unprepared, and that's why he lost. That may be, but almost every other opponent knew who he was, how tough of a fighter he was, and didn't give themselves a chance before they entered the ring with him. Buster was different. For some reason he stood his ground, and then began to take ground away from his fearsome opponent.

Buster explained later that he was in a different frame of mind, because of the very recent death of his mother. Ah! That's the key to his success: he had a **need** to not be shamed and embarrassed by his opponent, but instead, to exhibit honor and pride in memory of, and dedication to his dearly loved mother. Friends, Buster could have beat King Kong on that night!

Talent can get you in the ring but The Zone is sure to prevail—proceed with caution

Again, the power of **need** as a key to gain entry into The Zone.

Need: Real or Perceived

When your brain is confronted with a *real or perceived need*, it is programmed to forge the pathways between neurons to execute action, and satisfy that need. Imagine you hear a threatening noise inside your home at night. That perception will trigger your brain to get your heart pumping—pronto—mind planning, and body moving!

It appeared (remember I am sharing some conclusions from my research), that during Tiger's dominant period, he had a hunger to win that reached the intensity of a crisis need. Hence, it would answer the requirement of a high quality (pure) need, a real perceived *need*, as opposed to a want.

Have you ever gone without food long enough to know that you had to have something to eat right now? I'm sure we all know what it's like to have a full bladder, and need to find a rest room ASAP.

It is easy to understand why a wealthy athlete would not *need* to win a tournament. This is the nemesis of every successful person who performs for a living. The lifestyle lends itself to ease and luxury, yes "it is a lot of hard work," but it is still a game he or she would play for free every day of his/her life. "Need" is a hard level to maintain after you have reached the professional level, and consequently success—in any endeavor. Psychologist Abraham Maslow, in his popular *Hierarchy of Needs* even suggests: people go on the satisfy other needs once basic needs are met. So at some point the need for winning would fade.

It's also hard to feel like a failure or lose self-esteem when third place gets you $700,000, and a few top ten's will earn you a million or more for the season—welcome to professional golf. **Therefore, a period of rest from the intense pursuit, and a waning of the hunger (need) is understandable after the milestone of professional success is reached.**

So then, how is it that Tiger, and others like Sir Richard Branson, maintained the relentless pursuit from plateau to plateau to plateau? Although the contributing factors must be different among great performers, the level of need is the same. Kobe Bryant of the Los Angeles Lakers exhibits this same need. John McEnroe—the tennis icon—exhibited the same expectation to win every match.

If this is true, what we can learn from Tiger is probably true of others on his level, so let's examine more of what we know about his rise to and reign in golf.[5]

As The Demand, So The Power

I believe it was Sports Illustrated that ran an article several years ago during Tiger's early, dominant period. I am recalling this from memory, because I read this article in a waiting room, so don't hold me to *complete* accuracy; consider the fol-

---

[5] I am assuming Tigers tremendous, consistent performance demonstrated some level of the zone phenomenon based not only on his "highlight films" but percentage of wins to tournaments played.

lowing my recollection and interpretation. I wish I had savant type memory.

Need #1: Realized Potential

The key contributing factor, as I see it, is a desire to live up to his potential. You can pick any number of very successful, dominant athletes who exhibit the same qualities Ali, McEnroe, Tyson, Ruth, etc. This is a tremendous driver of need, because it is connected with self esteem, meaning, and purpose. Most of us have a strong desire to live up to our potential, so this is understandable. If you look at it from Tiger's perspective, he had world class potential, proven by a history of success against his peers as an amateur. To waste that would be simply demoralizing.

The expectations were very high from those who knew him, as well as those he imposed upon himself. So the need to prove himself against the best in the same way he did as an amateur, had to be great.

Need #2: Overcome (Need Hardened by Opposition)

The sports magazine article mentioned a fact that I was not aware of at the time, but I'm convinced was a significant factor in Tiger's intensity and drive. The article pointed out that Tiger required more security while playing golf than any professional golfer on the PGA tour in history. This was a shock to me, because I didn't notice that level of security while watching the tournaments; but do recall uniformed, armed officers escorting him from tee to tee in the early days.

The PGA tour usually has security at all of its events to

protect the players and fans from potentially rowdy fanatics and other incidents. Most of them are plain clothed. You will rarely see uniformed officers escorting a player from hole to hole, but I remember seeing this with Tiger in the early years, and shortly after the recent scandal.

I guess, because I was new to the game, I assumed it was normal protection for top golfers. Well, in fact, according to the article, it was due to death threats, and other threats of harm he was constantly receiving from some within the golf community; notably, after he won the *Masters* tournament for the first time. They were serious enough to warrant the PGA and the courses he played to increase visible, armed security, to assure peace and safety.

I also recall Nike (his main sponsor), running a full page ad in a national newspaper in an attempt to overcome known racism on the tour at the time Tiger became a professional. It was reported that at least one golf course on the professional tour at the time had a "whites only" policy, or at least discriminated against minorities.

Now, in my opinion, this is where a *desire* would transform into a *tremendous* need. We know what adrenaline does—it kicks in, so that if the option to run is not available, or desired, you are prepared to make "one mighty" stand—the old fight or flight response.

I am suggesting, the opposition Tiger Woods received, forced him to meet the threat with *more than* equal force. Apparently for him, the run option was off the table. He had to (metaphorically speaking) break the legs of his opposition to prevent their forward progress. This is a meet deadly force with deadlier force response.

I know it may seem extreme, but this is not the only time in history fans have threatened death upon a hated athlete. Later in the chapter titled *Idols, Heroes, and Fanatics*, we will look at Roger Maris, the home-run king's very similar situation. History records many more similar stories. Fanatics can be violently irrational at times.

I am sure Tiger was compelled to play with all of his *might* until it became obvious that he could not be denied or easily defeated; and that resolve he proved in a remarkably convincing way, as did Roger Maris at his time, and many others who faced similar opposition. Unfortunately, for the opposition, they often underestimate the potential of their target, under a "do or die", back to the wall circumstance. (If you're going to back a man into a corner, be sure to calculate your odds in a *fight*, in case he rejects the *flight* option.)

This element of additional opposition is a possible explanation for the difference between Tiger and other similarly gifted athletes, such as Phil Mickelson. I believe Phil is equally talented a golfer as Tiger when it comes to mastery of technique and knowledge of the game. But, the professional level requires you to bring everything you have, to every competition. That's a tough task, and I believe it goes **beyond the** *"mental game"* to the *"need game."*

Once you reach your destination, it's hard to conjure up a need if it's not real. "It's time to take a break from the climb," says the mind and body of the accomplished individual. Even a glutton for success may not be able to stuff more in his belly—and understandably so. Perhaps it's time to enjoy the fruits of labor, and utilized those gluttonous reserves of energy producing fatness in another of life's important endeavors.

Ask Pádraig Harrington (pro golfer), Erne Els (pro golfer), the Williams sisters, and any number of gifted athletes who know what it's like to ascend Mount Everest, to the top of the sports world. The fans, media, and sponsors demand more, but it is hard when you've arrived at the destination, are well fed, and facing an army of starving competition making their own climb to the top.

Although I'm discussing this within the context of "voluntary access" to The Zone, it is evident this level of need is very hard to generate from merely internal motivation, but usually is influenced by external factors (opposition), creating a type of threat response from the brain. This fact would add an "involuntary" aspect to this level of need, hence the undeniable *un-conscious* influence. Because this type of need is a direct act of the will (need), and the person is fully aware of what is happening, I am classifying it as voluntary.

Need that Crushes Mediocrity!

I remember the news coverage of the NFL's Dion Sanders induction into the *Hall of Fame*. In the clip I saw, he was explaining with passion that with every bit of opposition from the media or fans, he would see his mother struggling in poverty to provide for his family. That vision would propel him forward to greater achievements, and a **more powerful determination** to reach a level that would shatter poverty in his family, crush his opposition, and provide rest and relief to his beloved mother.

Again, the power of *real* need on the road to The Zone—whether it originates from within, or is coerced form without.

This is an essential key—**how bad do you NEED it?**

MAXIMUM POTENTIAL

A Need to See

The incredible ability of the brain to *make a way* in the face of impossibility—because of the *need* to perform—is powerfully demonstrated in the true story of the young man named Ben Underwood (introduced in chapter 4). Underwood developed a type of sonar sense, which allowed him to see objects around him, even though he was completely blind. This story is relevant to our discussion, because we are talking about the brain's potential—witnessed in glimpses during TZP.

This true story is one of those I would compare to the impact and significance of tornado and meteor strikes. It can't be ignored, and should be understood for what it means for you and me.

This story is not about how we all have the latent ability to use echo location. It's about brain *potential*—what the brain is *capable of when it is in complete control,* triggered by some definite need. In this story, out of sheer necessity, Underwood's brain was able to use the senses of hearing and speech, along with mathematics (a natural sense of size and distance relationships between objects), to make up for the loss of his eyesight.

The question naturally arises as to why he is one of a few human beings, we are aware of, to develop this unlearned ability at such an astonishing level of expertise.

Underwood's mother, Aquanetta Gordon, is credited with having a powerful influence on his maturity as a young man, and his ability to adapt to his circumstances. I have no doubt this credit is well deserved. Because, when as a blind two year old, Ben stated he couldn't see, and was frightened about the future, his mom **insisted** he **could** see the world. She told him nothing was impossible for him: "I tell him he can see," she said. She convinced him he could see with his hands, mouth, nose, and ears. The result of her influence and conviction is felt in Ben's words, "Ain't nothing wrong with me." **The *directive or command* from the mind and will, cause the brain to find a path to accomplishment.**

Another key to Underwood's transcendence was the absence of stifling fear, which his mother refused to invite to the table. We'll consider negative hindrances in more detail in the next chapter. But, I have to point out here, the fact that authority figures in a young life can and do have a tremendous influence, positive or negative, on shaping the beliefs and abilities of those young ones who depend on them.

IF NEED IS IMPORTANT CAN IT BE MANUFACTURED?

The Brain Knows Genuine Need

It is hard to manufacture need because of the trigger. Our brain is smarter than we are, and has to handle all of the body's functions, non-stop, 24/7, all of our life. So, if you attempt to convince yourself that scoring the next point or reaching the next milestone is an urgent, life or death, do or die situation, your brain is likely to be the judge of that.

I stated on page 198, that if you could look into the hearts of high achieving, but less then "great" performers, you would find their "strongest needs" are elsewhere. **It is unlikely (as I hope to have proven) the brain will easily allow itself to confuse wants with needs. The survival of the person depends on it.**

The great chess champion Bobby Fischer has insights on this topic, which we'll discuss in chapter 9. Suffice it to say: where your heart is, your needs, and therefore your efforts, will reside.

Extreme Sports: Need to Survive

"Through years of practice, a long way I've come. It might look easy, but don't try this at home" —jw

Rock climbing, cave diving, aerobatics, motocross, skydiving, wing-suit flying, free running, parkour, etc., are some of the sports in the extreme category. The common denominator in this category of athletic performance is danger, risk, and adrenalin consumption.

I am fascinated with extreme sport athletes who engage in dangerous sports with constantly changing variables such as speed, gravity, and weather conditions, which require adjustments and calculations to be made on the fly—in fractions of a second. There is an argument to be made for the assumption that these athletes must practically live in The Zone. Their concentration must be unflappable. Decisions must be quick and precise. Their level of physical fitness must be very high. Their knowledge and training must be thorough, so that their brains have a library of information to access when needed.

They make their accomplishments look easy, but the extremist has no doubt trained his brain to realize the *critical need* for precise execution.

> *"It's in my heart to love the trill, challenge the extremes, and test my skills. I know for a fact: I can conquer this. I am no fool...this is calculated risk."* —jw

The Value of Want?

Have I just minimized the idea of *wanting* personal success? Is "want" a powerless sentiment? Not exactly; but we are looking for maximum potential. To "want" is no worthless possession, as it is plentiful in the region adjacent to The Zone, where the feasting is good, but it can't unlock the gate to The Zone.

What Can Savant Phenomenon Teach Us?

We have seen how a clear directive from a **definite need** causes the brain to produce the phenomenal performance of The Zone. There is yet another similar **key** to unlock The Zone: a few characteristics which all savants have in common, tell us something about how their brains work, and therefore may give us insight into our own.

THE ONE TRACK MIND

Savants do at least one thing extremely well. That is an understatement. They do that thing with super natural proficiency. But, nearly every other task or ability suffers greatly. This is the part that causes most people to become uncomfortable, and shy away from savants, because they focus on the glaring disabilities instead of the gift.

This is the part that fascinates me most. Savants, for the most part, and geniuses also, have a gift in a very narrow field. For example, the gift is usually in math, music, art, and dates and time. Or like "The Rain Man," the rare ability to recall anything he has ever read.

With some exceptions, these individuals have to be cared for like children because they cannot function as other adults in the regular routines of life. Dressing themselves or cooking is outside of their abilities. Some savants (50%) are considered mentally handicap or autistic.

This "one track mind" should not be a surprise because we are all unable to do more than one thing at a time with precision, unless the two tasks are connected in a series, or are complimentary. For example, we can read and type, play piano and sing. When I sorted mail for UPS, I was able to read labels, and sort small packages into bins at a very high rate, while at the same time singing a favorite song (it helped my rhythm). On the other hand, I can't write this book and play an effective game of chess at the same time. *When it comes to high performance, we must focus our attention.*

Magicians are very aware of this tendency of the brain, and make their living with illusions designed to take advantage of the brain's reluctance to concentrate on more than one thing at a time. They have mastered the art of distraction, capitalizing on the brain's inclination to fixate. It is amazing and unsettling to become aware of how much information you miss that is right in front of you.

"It's hard to think critically if you're laughing, and keep the trickery outside the frame," are two of several secrets to magic, shared in the *"cognitive experiment in perception,"* by Teller—

the "silent" half of the famous Las Vegas act *Penn & Teller*, in a Readers Digest article.[6]

Our brain appears to be designed to focus proficiently, but multi-task not as well. This is a concept known very well, but not thoroughly explained, by many motivational and success gurus. "Set a goal and focus on it," is the usual, time tested exhortation. And many anecdotal examples of focused achievement are offered. "There is power in a single minded purpose to catapult you to success." "Have a clear cut objective," etc...

The Savant Brain

Well, this is indeed true, and the savant proves it, emphatically—however, with a downside. The savant's brain has directed, for reasons we don't fully understand, much of its resources to one specific area of interest. This includes his perception, understanding, memory, and sometimes motor functions, such as drawing or playing an instrument—every available brain resource works together in harmony toward the one specialized area of interest.

Their brains are either not able, or willing, or both to spend much time on anything else. It is as though their brains have decided to handle all of the necessary functions for life (heartbeat, immune function, body temperature, balance, etc.), and just *one more thing*. When it comes to the variable, non-essential areas of life, interacting with the world around them, the brain will focus on just one narrow area. The result? A super natural (beyond normal) performance, unreal exploits, mind blowing feats—The Zone of transcendence.

[6] http://www.rd.com/true-stories/inspiring/magic-tricks-revealed-by-teller-7-ways-to-fool-the-brain/2/

So, you can see where I'm going here: the savant represents the far end of the brain-potential spectrum—as far as we can contemplate. I can only imagine any human ability beyond this would be something easily recognized as god-like.

The fact that injury is usually the cause of this phenomenon doesn't minimize its significance for everyone (in my opinion), because the potential for extraordinary performance has to be there in the first place for it to surface. The fact that an accident is the spark doesn't matter—it just means something good has resulted from something bad. The potential for good has to be present to begin with.

Savant and Zone Comparison

The Zone Phenomenon likewise has an involuntary aspect, but, is fleeting in duration. Yet, in this state the brain has also taken a very narrow focus, and allocated most of its resources to that narrow area. The subject experiencing TZP is *forced to focus* on that task, while being only partially aware of what is going on around him. This is a step down (a momentary "day dream" for those who experience The Zone.) from the savant experience, which is for them a way of life.

The epitome—I speculate—would be a voluntary—at will—savant level performance, and a voluntary return to the normal world as seen in some fictitious comic book super hero characters. Like Batman or Superman who can put on a costume anytime they need super performance.

Some savants exhibit a genius knowledge or ability in an area of which they are unfamiliar, while others are incredible learners of new things. This adds another level as to what the epitome would look like—instant knowledge, and endless capacity for rapid learning.

I am reminded of the scene in *The Matrix* movie where the fictitious *Neo* receives a mental download, making it possible for him to rapidly become a master of Kung Fu. Fascinating! Many savants don't need to download anything; as far as we know, they *instantly know* wonderful things. However, for the rest of us, it appears, all we can expect to experience is the occasional "drafting into" The Zone, and the inevitable ejection back to reality, as providence would have it.

KEY: We are able to ascertain from what we just discussed, that the brain will perform at a high level when it is **focused** like a laser beam (single minded proficiency), triggered by a **demand** often accompanied by a tremendous **need** for super human performance.

Now that we have identified the road or paths to The Zone, and keys to entry, let's identify the barriers, roadblocks, pitfalls, obstacles, and such, along the road—those known, overlooked, and newly discovered hindrances to entry and permanent Zone residence.

CHAPTER SEVEN

Roadblocks, Obstacles, Barriers & Pitfalls

"A double minded man is unstable
in all of his ways"
—James

A ll roadblocks, obstacles, barriers, and pitfalls, will not only prevent you from entering The Zone to begin with, but will expel you once you are there. Some obstacles, you meet along the road, while others are self-imposed. I am convinced that many of us are needlessly frustrated with our ability to excel in our chosen endeavor. Needless, because we are either doing things which work against us, effectively constructing a barrier to our goals; or neglecting to do things which are necessary for success. One thing is certain—no goal is accomplished automatically (excepting a brief, fortuitous, involuntary Zone invitation. But that's like waiting on lightning to strike you). We have to put forth effort to make our goals happen. As we will see, our plan of action needs to include not just positive steps, but preventative measures to reduce the likelihood of being derailed by negative forces.

IMPAIRMENTS

As we have seen, the brain sets about its chore of managing and regulating body tasks and functions, so that they are all carried out in the easiest way possible, and ultimately become automatic.

When a process is impaired by something that disrupts the flow of communication between neurons in the network, things will go wrong, and the task will not be performed correctly or efficiently; little chance of proficiency. If the task is performed, it will either not be with normal ease and speed, or it will be performed incorrectly with errors in the process. We saw a clear picture of the effects of impairment in the previous chapter when we discussed how therapy helps us recover from injury.

This chapter is designed to identify and help remove a number of common obstacles to maximum brain and body performance.

Natural Impairment

The most common—overlooked and unavoidable—impairment to optimal human performance is *aging*. All of our legendary heroes: sports, music, and other outstanding performers, prove this fact. Unfortunately as we get older, our cells (with an apparent expiration date), no longer repair and replicate as well as they once did. We know this as getting old. The once sharp eyesight becomes blurry, the muscles weaken, bones become fragile, hearing needs aid, and so on. Generally, we reach our physical performance peak somewhere around the age of 25, then plateau until around 35; after that, the slow process of biological deterioration begins, until finally we expire.[1] Not trying to be morbid, but these are the facts of life on planet earth. To be forewarned is to be forearmed.

Any time these impairments arise, they *will* have a negative effect on our performance. I would call this kind of obstacle to extraordinary, or even optimal, performance—natural, inevitable, at some point in our lifetime—impairments.

With this knowledge, we should plan our journey to, and sojourn in The Zone carefully, and adjust our expectations accordingly. And for sure, not do anything willfully to speed up the arrival of this impending impairment.

But, as sure as we as a species have proven unable to avoid harm to ourselves, many of us will ignore this warning, and hasten the onset of this category of impairment to your physical and mental performance. Smoking and heavy drinking, for instance, are known to speed up the aging process, as well as our expiration date. I will write more on this shortly.

Physical injury can also be an unavoidable impairment or obstacle to maximum performance. Although many have used it as a catalyst for phenomenal performance (autistic savants are a good example). Likewise, many defy age impairment. Jack Lalanne, George Foreman, and Tom Watson (the golfer), are good examples of **age defying physical performance**.

Voluntary Impairment

A familiar and powerful example of **self inflicted impairment** is driving under the influence of drugs or alcohol—or

---

[1] Aging And Exercise, Roy j. Shephard, sportsci.org/encyc/agingex/agingex.html

any performance under the influence. **These conditions provide a very good example of just how delicate and sensitive the communication networks between our brain cells are.**

After we have learned to drive, the task becomes automatic, like walking, or riding a bicycle, we don't have to think about it. Most of us reach a level of proficiency and confidence, allowing us to multi-task while performing this potentially dangerous task (I know this is debatable, but stay with me). The brain has made it easy and automatic.

Now, when you add intoxication to the task, from drugs or alcohol—all of a sudden—what was once a simple task becomes extremely difficult to perform properly, without endangering yourself and everyone else on the road.

What has happened? We have interfered with the chemical and electrical signals, which normally come into play when we call on our brain to manage that task, which it has previously mastered. The brain's control of speech and motor function has become impaired. **The transmission of information between the neurons and muscles has been short-circuited by the addition of a strong contaminating chemical, causing malfunction.**

Most other bodily processes decrease in priority when this kind of substance enters the bloodstream in high quantities, and reaches vital organs. This protective reaction occurs in the liver (the body's primary filter against harmful chemicals), where alcohol receives priority treatment, as much as is possible, in a *fight* to prevent death from poisoning.[2] For the alcoholic, the liver sometimes loses its valiant fight against cirrhosis early. In the mean time, the body, brain, and physical

---

[2] See Understanding Nutrition, By Ellie Whitney, Eleanor Noss Whitney, Sharon Rady Rolfes, 2011, p. 234

performance, suffer from malnourishment and impairment when drugs enter the body.

We may not be aware of our body's systems and functions beings neglected, until the neglect reaches a critical level, and we are forced to rest (as in go to bed,) while the body commits every resource to fight the threat and regain health. Been sick lately? Ever seen a intoxication induced comatose sleep?

Clogged Arteries

Artery: a main channel or highway, especially of a connected system with many branches.

It is easy to understand the importance of keeping the communication pathways between neurons clear and uncontaminated, if we are to experience anything close to Zone-like mental and physical performance. How many otherwise talented individuals were derailed and crippled by this self induced impairment...substance abuse?

Some of you may think of your favorite rock star and say: "Hey, he is still going strong after years of drug abuse." But only he knows the extent of his ailments and impairments. You won't know them unless the entertainer shares them. I can assure you the entertainer with the heavy drug past is not in the condition (for their age) that Jack Lalanne (the health/fitness guru) was at the age of 90.

So, if you want to perform at peak potential as you grow older, I would suggest you follow Jack Lalanne's example, not the fabulous entertainer who's destroying brain cells, and working his liver to death.

"Well, you're gonna' die from something," "When it's your

time, it's your time!" Yes, there is some truth to those sentiments, *but you might live with something*—for a long time at that. Have you seen anyone lately waiting for an organ transplant, or living with no voice box due to **self** impairment?

Nutrition

While we are on the subject of ingesting harmful substances, let's look at what we eat, and how it affects our performance. I am amazed at how many otherwise educated people don't understand the role of food in human health and performance. Many *refuse* to believe what I'm about to share.

Diet plays a vital role in our ability to perform at maximum efficiency, because everything we eat and drink is converted into chemical form by our digestive system, and then distributed to waiting organs and cells through our blood stream. Those wonderful cells we talked about a few chapters ago don't make their own food for energy and proper function—we supply it by eating. This sounds like a simple concept, yet many of us live as though the only purpose for eating and drinking is to satisfy hunger cravings—in the most pleasurable way possible. They have little knowledge or care for the fact that hunger is triggered by **need** for the **nourishment** of our cells. It's another one of those marvelous processes in which the brain plays an important role.

No wonder the hospitals are the fastest growing institutions in the world.

Those tiny mitochondria (the cells motorized power generators we mentioned on page 35), release *energy* by converting *nutrients* into explosive chemical energy. They **need** fatty acids, amino acids, and simple sugars (not refined junk food sugar,) to function properly. If you are eating properly, your mitochondria will have the *tools* to **energize** you—up from your cells, out through your entire body! Need some get-up-and-go? You now know where to start.

While we are on this subject, some advice: be skeptical of *magic pill* remedies. Because proper body function is a co-operative process between all systems. No single part holds all the power. This is why (natural) nutrition provides such a powerful punch. Veggies, fruits, and such are packed with a variety of nutrients (many not even known). Let them be your magic pill for optimal physical and mental performance.

So, if you are in a malfunction state? In this case one of low energy. It is likely to take some time to restore your system to full strength through the repair process that begins with proper and adequate nutrition. That is not likely to happen overnight—except for a miracle.

Feed Your Brain

Our brain is the biggest consumer of blood in our bodies, circulating about a quart of blood every minute. Therefore, it is easy to see why it is so quickly affected by what goes into our mouths—good or bad.

All drug, legal or illegal, are designed to produce a powerful affect in the body. All of the drugs we consume eventually circulate through the brain's **100,000 miles of blood vessels.** The effects of good drugs like aspirin, or bad ones like alcohol, can be noticed in a matter of minutes. Your digestive system is *very proficient* at delivering whatever you ingest throughout your body, especially your brain. Are you feeling mentally sluggish? What are you digesting?

Food is responsible for supplying the proteins and amino acids the brain needs to produce the neurotransmitters (communication molecules) like endorphins, dopamine, and serotonin, which are responsible for creating a sense of well being (mental and psychological balance) and happiness. These brain chemicals influence your behavior as well as mood. For example, in the evening when your brain chemical melatonin is high, you begin to feel sleepy. If your serotonin level is high, one of the effects is you are **not** likely to be depressed, but rather enjoy a sense of well being. If your dopamine is low, among other things, you will likely feel unhappy. If you have "mind altering" drugs in your system the delicate balance is thrown off, and a host of negative psychological, physical, and behavioral problems will eventually result.

Chemical dependency results from the brain stopping its own neurotransmitter production, because the drug creates a *false* condition of too much of the similar brain chemical. If the drug mimics dopamine, the brain says "Too much dopamine!" then stops production. The victim becomes unhappy when the drug wears off, and goes for another hit of the drug...and the vicious cycle repeats over and over again. I am simplifying what can be a complex cycle, as different classes of mind and mood altering drugs have different effects.

Another important point to remember is that, unlike most other cells in the human body, **brain cells do not repair themselves after they are damaged**. Therefore, any activity that will destroy brain cells such as inhaling chemicals (inadvertently or to get high) is a form of suicide or at least brain damage. The brain cells you destroy are most certainly important for maximum performance, or they wouldn't have been there to begin with. (There is current talk about neurogenesis but no evidence exists that new brain cells grow in any significant quantity or actually replace damaged neurons.)

Considering we are masterfully assembled living beings, we wouldn't dare think we could deliberately cut off an appendage, so why would we believe we could afford to lose a few hundred thousand brain cells? Interestingly enough, many adolescents (I was one), and adults—after being warned that one of the negative results of "huffing" is the destruction of brain cells—respond with an attitude that suggests, they have brains cells to spare. "If I can't immediately *feel* the negative side effects, it can't be that serious," they reason. The consequences may not be seen right away, but the damage is certainly occurring. If we didn't need 100 billion brain cells would we be born with them? Can you really *thrive* with a few billion less?

In her book *The Mood Cure*, Julie Ross, M.A. makes a very strong case for the importance of eating good quality proteins, so as to provide the raw material the body, brain, and cells, need to produce balanced mood, good sleep, and an overall healthy frame of mind. She is careful to also point out the destructive effects of "bad mood" junk foods. Bottom line is that what goes into your mouth or enters your blood stream will either help you or impair you on the road to maximum potential! You can be certain that if your brain is disabled by over-saturation of toxins, the rest of your body will suffer, and your performance will be diminished.[3]

Vitamins and Minerals

It has become common knowledge that vitamins and miner-

[3] Also see on my blog, The Brain our Universe-Matter (8 min. mark)

als are not only essential for the proper growth of our brain and body in the early stages of development, but continue to remain vital for proper function of our bodies as we age.

"Maternal vitamin C deficiency during pregnancy can have serious consequences for the fetal brain. And once brain damage has occurred, it cannot be reversed by vitamin C supplements after birth."[4]

The above quoted university study goes on to say that *"10-20% of all adults in the developed world suffer from vitamin C deficiency."* This is just one *vital* nutrient and its affect on human performance.

Lack of vital nutrients is detrimental at the *cellular level* of our bodies, and will *eventually* result in some malfunction along the pathways for accomplishing necessary tasks. To use a common metaphor, if you don't change the oil in your engine, lube the joints, and use good quality gas to run your car, you are asking for a malfunction—even more so with our precious physical bodies, that require special fuel for maintenance and optimal, lifelong performance.

The best source of these vital nutrients is **living foods,** which our bodies recognize, and easily digest into useful chemicals. Eat your fruits, veggies, grains, and good quality meats, as fuel for maximum sustained Zone performance. Or, sooner or later suffer the consequences of mediocrity and ill health.

Sugar

I can't help but emphasize the one overused, common sub-

[4] University of Copenhagen (2012, November 16). Fetus suffers when mother lacks vitamin C. Science Daily. Retrieved April 9, 2013, from http://www.sciencedaily.com /releases/2012/11/121116085629.htm

stance (of which I have in recent years become more aware) that has negative effects on the body systems, and brain function. That substance is *refined* sugar, which according to many nutritional experts, has a drug-like, addictive effect on the brain. Refined sugar is not the naturally occurring "simple sugar" we find in fruit, but is a man-made (or altered) chemical. I mention it because it is not a positive *nutrient*, yet is ingested in incredible quantities in our culture.

Refined sugar is cited by experts[5] as a primary contributor to emotional problems in children and adults often diagnosed with mood and behavioral disorders.

> *"...Dr. Martin classified refined sugar as a poison because it has been depleted of its life forces, vitamins and minerals...Incomplete carbohydrate metabolism results in the formation of 'toxic metabolite' such as pyruvic acid...Pyruvic acid accumulates in the brain and nervous system...These toxic metabolites interfere with the respiration of the cells. They cannot get sufficient oxygen to survive and function normally. In time, some of the cells die. This interferes with the function of a part of the body and is the beginning of degenerative disease."[6]*

Simply put, refined sugar causes cells to malfunction and die, causing disease.

Are we (recipients of the highest level of intelligence on earth) going to allow a finite *poisonous* molecular substance like refined sugar to derail our potential, and imprison us— taking its toll on our minds and bodies? There is help. Julie Ross, (in *The Mood Cure*) recommends a few key nutrients,

---

[5] Including "The Mood Cure" by Julie Ross
[6] Article Written by William Dufty, Why Sugar Is Toxic To The Body http://www.globalhealingcenter.com/sugar-problem/refined-sugar-the-sweetest-poison-of-all

usually lacking in those who suffer from addictive sugar cravings. (You'll have to pick up a copy of her book to find out which nutrients.)

You say, "Addict?! Who are you talking about?" Well, have you ever tried to *free yourself* from refined sugar? I did. And l can tell you, I was shocked at how much of a sugar junky I am. I ended up settling on half water and half juice to start my liberation, (couldn't go cold turkey, needed some kind of sweet drink,) before finally being able to enjoy plain, pure water. I now rarely drink packaged fruit juice. In exchange, I prepare my own juice using raw fruits, vegetables, and water. My overall health and performance have improved tremendously. Not to mention my weight is normal for a healthy person my age. I am now turning my attention to ridding myself of the frequent craving for dessert.

Signs of Sugar Addiction

Most of us have experienced an inability to relax after consuming a large quantity of a refined sugar product. There is such a thing as a "sugar high." We know this, and therefore, on a regular basis reach for sugar as an emotional or physical picker-upper. The sweet liquid drinks are the easiest to consume, and with as much as 34,000 milligrams (34 grams) of sugar, they pack a serious punch. If you are like me, and have taken dietary supplements, you are familiar with 500-1,000 milligram tablets. Can you fathom taking 34 tablets at a time? Well, the refined sugar in one soft or sports drink is usually equal to 34 x 1,000 milligram tablets, which is a mega dose prescription for a sugar junkie. Check the label!

Now, if your goal is the relaxed concentration required

in The Zone, then a high sugar diet with its drug like effects would certainly derail your efforts. This is a **huge roadblock**. There are probably millions who would not need sleeping pills if they cut refined sugar out of their diets.

Incidentally, in spring time 2012, for the first time in my life, I heard national news reports citing studies warning of the toxic and addictive effects of sugar on the human brain and body. *Natural* health professionals have been warning about this for decades.

Performance Enhancing Drugs

- Lance Armstrong Lied, Cheated, Doped...
- Athletics: Olympic champion Kuzenkova banned for doping...
- Olympic champion Cakir Alptekin faces possible life-time athletics ban...
- Barry Bonds and Baseball's Doping Scandal...
- Track star Marion Jones pleads guilty to doping deception...

And so the headlines read. There are too many occurrences of drug enhanced athletic performance to list here. Athletes from every country under heaven are on the list, and these are the ones who were caught.[7]

The music industry is notorious for the use of drugs. From Rappers to hard rockers, every genre has a history of drug use. Hollywood actors have the same reputation. I am certain many of these performers use drugs to "enhance their

---

[7] http://en.wikipedia.org/wiki/List_of_doping_cases_in_athletics

performance", whether it's simply to keep up a hectic pace or go to sleep. Back to this shortly.

There are at least two sides to this issue:

1. Drugs for enhancement of human performance are morally wrong because they give an unfair advantage to the competitors who use them.

2. Science has the right, moreover, the obligation to contribute to the world's understanding of our bodies, and when possible the improvement of our performance.

We see this debate occur almost exclusively in the realm of sports completion, where the ethical idea of unfair advantage is very well represented.

This book is about human potential, so do you expect me to argue against anything that would expose human deficiencies in performance, and contribute to the realization of latent potential? Well, for me this is a dilemma, but my answer is, yes I may argue against it, and no I may not argue against it.

Let's take the negative side first. I just mentioned Lance Armstrong the incredible cyclist who dominated his opponents. Barry Bonds *over conquered* the conquest of Mark McGuire. Marion Jones, the Olympic super star runner, and other champion athletes have proved that human beings are functioning (on a normal level) below our potential. These athletes have proven: medical science—to a significant degree—has knowledge and capability to nudge mankind up the ladder toward maximum potential.

Are we supposed to ignore or reject this advancement in science, and accept a normality we know to be mediocre? If there were truly a "drug" like the one depicted in the recent movie *Limitless,* which could give everyone a "Rain Man" like memory, do you think it would be banned on the bases of creating an unfair advantage in the academic and business environment?

Potential personal harm to the athlete is a separate issue with its own moral question of: how much authority does anyone else have over what a person does with their own body? Also, when it comes to ingesting harmful substances, where would the authorities draw the line of prohibition? We just have to read the labels on most of our packaged food products, and research a few ingredients to confirm many ingredients are not meant for human consumption, and are identified as harmful to the human body. The point is, from candy to Prozac, most of us are free to consume harmful substances without judgment or condemnation.

Why isn't ingesting electrolytes through sports drinks *adding an advantage*...shouldn't pure water be the only liquid allowed during competition to assure a level playing field?

I'm not necessarily saying a line shouldn't be drawn somewhere. But who will draw it, and where it should be drawn, so as to avoid the accusation of hypocrisy, is a difficult question to answer. Who would condone potentially harmful drugs for some, and ban them for others?

Lucy in the Sky with Diamonds

This human performance enhancing dilemma is further complicated when we broaden our discussion to include the idea of mind altering drugs. The idea is to improve the performance of the brain and mind through drugs, so that the senses (sight, sound, touch, smell, and imagination) can be heightened: taken from a low functioning state to a higher one.

Drugs were thought to contribute to the genius of "great" hard-rock acts like Jimmy Hendricks, Janice Joplin, The Beatles, Queen, Michael Jackson, etc., who no doubt "expanded their creativity" through the use of mind altering drugs, to which many fans contribute their extremely successful albums (like Queen's Bohemian Rhapsody). In case you are unaware, the title of this section comes from a popular Beatles song purported to refer to the drug LSD.

Native Americans have used the extract from a popular cactus in religious ceremonies for over 3,000 years. In 1954 Aldous Huxley wrote a popular essay *The Door of Perception* about his experience with a "trip", induced by the extract. In the epilogue to his novel *The Devils of London*, published earlier that year, Huxley had written that drugs were "toxic short cuts to self-transcendence."[8] Although I haven't read Huxley's essay or book, excerpts indicate his expectations were greatly disappointed. This leads us to the argument against the use of synthetic (artificial) performance enhancers.

Historically drugs demonstrate their harmful effects on the human body, and often cause death. There is something here to be said for the body's desire/fight for homeostasis (the efforts of the body to maintain internal stability, balance, and harmony.) This fact also contributes to my conclusions at the end of the book: "What is it that prevents us from living up to our true potential? Why is "homeostasis" fixed below our true potential?"

The dysfunctional lives and death of many "great" performers is proof that their drug use caused a physiological

[8] http://en.wikipedia.org/wiki/The_Doors_of_Perception

imbalance which contributed to early decline and subsequent expiration.

No matter what experts say about performance enhancing substances, it appears the human body has a natural aversion to them. This includes psychiatric drugs which often produce "zombie-like" function in those who take them. There is a lot more to this story, so you may be interested in the documentary on my blog after you finish this chapter.[9]

After witnessing a childhood friend, and seeing others *"lose their mind"* after a "bad trip", I personally have a very strong aversion to anything with the potential of taking over the driver's seat of my brain and mind. All it takes is one mistake and you are consciously dead to this world. So, when it comes to enhanced human potential, I'll have to say no to drugs.

The Gut and Psychological Health

Your digestive system has a direct link to your brain, and therefore your emotional and psychological wellbeing, according to Dr. Natasha Campbell-McBride,[10] who writes and teaches on the subject, as well as treats patients in her clinic. For the record she is not alone in her conclusions.

As a result of her medical research on the connection between our digestive system and our brains, she was able to completely cure her young son and other children of autism. She did this through ***eliminating*** harmful, hard to digest

[9] http://un-conscious.com/videos// the-truth-about-psychotropic-drugs
[10] http://gaps.me/ Gut and Psychology Syndrome (GAP Syndrome or GAPS)™

foods (refined sugar was first) from his diet, and ***adding*** helpful, beneficial foods and supplements: chiefly probiotics. By the way, she points out, that if you have ever had antibiotics your digestive system is compromised, because the good bacteria (probiotics) will not replenish on their own, but must be re-introduced through foods high in these good microorganisms such as fermented foods and yogurt. Her research and knowledge is ground breaking, with proven results, and should be studied by everyone interested in answers to these ailments and the epidemic of mental, emotional, and psychological problems in our communities and families.

Of course, would-be Zone residents would be careful not to ignore this important knowledge, because, if *control central* (the brain) is impaired, you have little chance of maximum Zone-like performance.

McBride's findings are consistent with those of William Dufty's in 1975:

> ...Clinical research with hyperactive and psychotic children, as well as those with brain injuries and learning disabilities, has shown: "...that their systems cannot handle sugar; dependence on a high level of sugar in the diets of the very children who cannot handle it. "Inquiry into the dietary history of patients diagnosed as schizophrenic reveals the diet of their choice is rich in sweets, candy, cakes, coffee, caffeinated beverages, and foods prepared with sugar. These foods, which stimulate the adrenals, should be eliminated or severely restricted."[11]

My friends, these facts are in the *Basic Operators Manual*

---

[11] Sugar Blues, © 1975 by William Dufty quoting Hoffer, Abram, "Megavitamin B3 Therapy for Schizophrenia", Canadian Psychiatric Association Journal, vol. 16, 1971

for the human body: the *fundamental guide to human living and thriving on planet earth.* Somehow we have lost the instruction manual, and the result has been a generation or two of tremendous nutritional ignorance, resulting in many diseases caused by unhealthy eating.

Since we are discussing barriers to entering The Zone I have discussed nutrition, but keep in mind I am not a nutritionist or expert, (although I have studied, and continue to study a few.) Therefore, I encourage you to consult any of the books and blogs available on the subject. The few that I have mentioned are excellent.

Hydration

If what experts say is true: about the brain consisting of approximately 78% water, how important is it for us to drink enough pure water, and not make our bodies work so hard to extract water from soft drinks and juices? Your body doesn't produce water on its own; you have to deliberately supply it. What are the possible health consequences for many who rarely drink pure water...how efficient is their brain function?

Dehydration

I mentioned a few paragraphs ago that I had trouble weaning myself from sugar, and tried watering down my fruit juice. I recently came across the published work of Dr. F. Batmanghelid who wrote the book *The Water Cure.* His claims have been criticized by some as extreme, but I'm interested in recognizing obvious truth, and weighing the value of conclusions reached by the doctor. All things considered, his warnings can't be ignored. His book maintains, that his research and experience indicate most Americans are dehydrated, because we simply don't drink enough pure water.

Well, we know the cells in our body need nutrients to accomplish the manufacturing work they perform (see chapter 3), and the chief nutrient is water—so plentiful, yet so scarce, in our day and time.

I can't go into all I've learned in my research, but suffice it to say, after being convinced by the Doctor's advice, I began to drink more water—whether I feel thirsty or not—and found my energy level increase. I also noticed other positive changes in my body. For example, the aid to my adrenal glands was the most appreciated benefit of increasing my pure water intake. I learned that the adrenal glands, sitting atop the kidneys, are dependent on sufficient supply of water to function properly.

For more on the symptoms of dehydration, and the necessity and benefits of pure water consumption, you can visit my blog or lookup *The Water Cure* by Dr. F. Batmanghelid on Youtube or Amazon.

Now, let's move from the self-induced *causes* of mental, emotional, and physical impairments to The Zone of transcendent human performance, to understanding the *manifestations* themselves.

PSYCHOLOGICAL OBSTACLES: FEAR AND DOUBT

First Things First: Make Sure You're Not The Cause

I believe I've established that the effects of impairments like narcotics and sugar on the brain can be responsible for the emotional and psychological obstacles we are about to discuss. That is why I began there. Faced with any of the following psychological obstacles, it's wise to **first:** eliminate roadblock #1 (*self impairment*) as the cause, before we consider any outside cause.

William Dufty *Sugar Blues*:

> *"Today, doctors all over the world are repeating what Tintera announced years ago: nobody, but nobody, should ever be allowed to begin what is called "psychiatric treatment", anyplace, anywhere, unless and until they have had a glucose tolerance test to discover if they can handle sugar."*

This point is very important, because we are not conditioned to look inward (especially not in our stomachs) when we experience emotions like fear, doubt, paranoia, depression, etc. Our first inclination is to identify who or what circumstances are causing these feelings. **Unfortunately, as life would have it, we can always find someone to blame for our emotional upsets, so we wage war in the wrong place.**

I am suggesting, we first look inward, to our own digestive system for substances *known and proven* to cause interference in the brain, and as a result distort our perception of reality, affect our feelings, as well as our *ability to cope with real* problems.

So then...assuming we have eliminated the self imposed impairments discussed in the previous section, fear and doubt along to path to maximum performance remain obstacles common to every healthy person, and must be dealt with.

> *"To fear is human, to overcome is necessary"*
> -jw

The Brain and Fear: The Shift to Auto Pilot

Fear is the one emotion that immediately sets the brain into autopilot. That is to say, **most options are taken out of our hands** from the time the brain is alerted by fear. The brain sets off a series of reactions in the body designed to prepare the person to either fight or escape the threat. This is a "survival instinct", and it's programmed into our DNA at our very core. Our brain requires no conscious, deliberate input from us, except for observation through our senses, before it takes complete control and alerts all defensive, offensive, and supporting forces, that a major threat has been detected—prepare for action!

Irrational Fear

Fear can be a good thing as we've noted, but a problem occurs when we experience *irrational* fear when there is no actual life threatening situation. This happens all too often in life. Many who have climbed the ladder to success experience the powerful presence of fear along the journey; which in hindsight is seen as irrational.

Let me illustrate this point with an example. If I am standing in the waiting room before a job interview, trembling, palms sweating, heart pounding, lungs expanding, muscles tensing—am I really afraid that the interviewer will hurt me?

The answer is yes, and my psychological and emotional state is proof. In that situation my fear is irrational, but my brain does not know this. My brain reacted to the directives I sent it through the way I *interpreted* the situation, and as a result triggered the series of responses it is programmed to trigger. Sadly, this will make it impossible for me to perform well, unless my desire is to run, in which case I have all the power I need to run from anticipated danger.

I have irrationally directed my brain to fear (i.e. she won't like you...we won't click etc.), through negative self talk ("don't blow it...that would be disaster"). The brain has prepared me for impending disaster by calling in the reinforcements to take over. I have become the irrational prisoner of fear, and all I really wanted was solid performance.

In this case, on the general journey toward success the fear which inhibits is often not triggered by observing something through our senses, but is triggered by our **imagination**. Sadly, the effects are the same. I recall my first radio interview after sending out a press release for my book project. I was very excited, but soon that excitement turned into fear. I still can't put my finger on exactly why I was so afraid. Needless to say I wasn't that sharp, in fact it was pretty bad. What happened?

Adrenalin

In response to fear, the brain initiates many actions, including increased heart rate, blood pressure, and respiration. These actions pump more blood to the muscles, which supplies more oxygen to the muscles and heart-lung system; *increases sugar rates in the blood*, which allow for rapid energy use, and accelerate the metabolism for emergency actions; *thickens the blood to increase oxygen supply* (red cells), which enables better defense from infections (white cells) and stops bleeding quickly (platelets); *sharpens the senses*—the pupils dilate, hearing is better, etc., allowing for rapid responses; *prioritizes increased blood supply to peripheral muscles and heart*, which targets the motor and basic-function regions in the brain; *decreases blood supply to digestive system and irrelevant brain regions* (such as speech areas), which causes secretion of body wastes, leaving the body lighter; *increases the secretion of adrenaline and other stress hormones*, which increases the response and strengthens relevant systems; and increases the secretion of endorphins, natural painkillers, providing an instant defense against pain. *(Atkinson et al, 1996; Hanson, 1986; Kandel, 1991)*

No wonder I was dazed and confused for hours after that short radio interview!

In life on planet earth, fear is rarely our friend, because it sets off much **too powerful** a chemical reaction in the body to allow normal, smooth, and fluid performance. Not to mention, it's hard to concentrate on anything other than coping with fear, once it is allowed to enter the situation. You will find yourself distracted by the powerful symptoms of fear itself.

Fear is a definite barrier to entering the high performance region of The Zone. It is a powerful roadblock. **Irrational fear is NOWHERE to be found in The Zone region.**

Rational Fear: Danger and the Brain

In a situation involving irrational fear, the person has summoned a real and powerful army for an imaginary war. But let's face reality, there are situations when the armed forces of adrenal response are needed and appreciated.

In the realm of human performance, some of these include extreme sports, dare devil stunts, and situations where something can potentially go dangerously wrong. Oh, and if you happen to be in the boxing ring with Mike Tyson, rational fear (alarm to danger) is a good thing produced by a healthy brain!

Fear vs. Terror

The serious mindset of extreme athletes, which may falsely be interpreted as fear, is actually a *respect* for the inherent dangers of their sport, combined with a high degree of concentration and focus, which **force the brain to restrict the performance options** to those successfully learned and practiced. The body must faithfully repeat the successful maneuvers it has previously learned. The *only* option is successful execution—Period.

This reaction corresponds to the "fight" side of our innate fear response. A serious awareness of danger is necessary to trigger the brain-controlled, adrenal-aided response needed for superior performance. Carelessness would be fatal. Instead of "flight", the extremist has chosen to *use* the **symptoms** of fear to overcome the danger or threat.

> *"It's in my heart to chase the thrills, challenge the extremes and test my skills. Through years of practice I've prepared for this. I am no fool—this is calculated risk" —jw*

For example, a tight rope walker is not afraid of walking that rope across a couple of buildings 500 feet in the air. Not to the extent he has set off the "flight" response we talked about. Now, if *you* tried to walk that rope, every last one of the chemical and physical reactions of fear would flood your body with **terror/panic**, and you would probably never complete the first step onto the rope. As a matter of fact, just looking out through the window would be enough to upset my stomach, weaken my knees, and stutter my speech—for starters.

But the experienced "dare devil" rope walker has a serious respect for the dangers involved, which alert his brain to meet the possible danger with a very high level of mental concentration and focus (another fear response), executing the task according to the maneuvers learned during study and training. The focus and concentration is so intense that it's difficult, if not impossible to deviate from the plan of action, because of the high risk of injury or death. **This is an example of harnessing your fear, or to be more descriptive: putting a saddle on your fear and riding it for all its worth.** True "fearlessness" would not only be *irrational,* but would not provide the extra power and focus needed to triumph. Fearlessness will impress a lot of people, but will leave you unprotected in the presence of danger.

> "Through years of practice; a long way I've come. It might look easy...but don't try this at home" —jw

Practice—Train—Learn

The understandable *unwillingness* of the brain to allow any deviation from the *best* path to safety is a good incentive for dare devils to practice Plan A and Plan B scenarios, and any reasonable "what if" scenarios. Remember how fast the brain processes information? **1 million, million, million calculations per second, occurring at 250 mph between neurons**—there is plenty of time to run through all options in just a single second. The old "life flashing in front of your eyes" is actually possible; in fact it's theoretically easy for the brain. (This is a critical part of the unconscious reliance on the brain to do what it is capable of doing.)

I have always admired jugglers. Their ability to juggle so many tasks at the same time amazes me, because it appears not to be enough time to catch all of those objects and throw them without dropping them. The talented juggler has a fine-tuned sense of **time** which allows him/her to make decisions and execute in fractions of a second. The extremist, likewise, has the same sense of time, as the brain executes dangerous maneuvers, and monitors options with precision, in split seconds.

I know training regimens for many potentially hazardous sports include practice on how to fall, so as to eliminate or reduce injury. Sky divers have a back-up parachute just in case, and scenarios for when to deploy it.

If contingency plans are included in training and practice, they can prevent a paralyzing fear-induced rush of adrenalin, possible panic, and allow the brain to keep thinking for solutions in the event of an emergency. I am not a military man, but I would guess elite soldiers are trained to anticipate every possible contingency and threat. **This kind of preparation can turn paralysis into positive action in the face of fear.** The same goes for preparation in civilian life. (Had I implemented this truth before my radio interview I would have experienced a more positive performance.)

I am amazed at how motor cross sports have evolved, especially the aerial acrobatics. In that sport today, these guys have learned to flip and twist those motor cycles in all kinds of ways, in the short amount of time it takes to jump from one mound of dirt to the other. It appears that over the years they have come to realize: that the brain and body are able to accomplish much more in a few seconds than we first believed possible. They have sliced those seconds into smaller and smaller pieces of potential maneuvers. It seems they are maximizing the brain's ability to do 1 million, million, million computations in a second. If a significant portion of this processing power is focused on maneuvering that motor cycle and the physical body, who knows what the limit will one day be.

THE FORKS IN THE ROAD

Doubt and similar situations, or should I say predicaments, are what I consider a barrier or roadblock. What are the effects of doubt (a close family member of fear) on our ability to remain in or enter The Zone?

In our discussion on the power of need as a key to The Zone (page 86), I introduced the Discovery Channel video series called *The Miraculous Mind*, which discussed the brains ability to heal and recover from damage caused by trauma.

We looked at plasticity—the brain's ongoing ability to learn new things, and forge new pathways. The ability to observe this brain process gives us a look into how the brain creates *all* knowledge and performance pathways.

You may be asking: what does this have to do with doubt and fear? I am about to forge the connection for you.

The dictionary defines doubt as: *to be uncertain about; consider questionable or unlikely; hesitate to believe, to distrust, to fear; be apprehensive about.*

Therapy: Demand A New Path

An injured person will begin to recover physically, **only** after the brain has begun to build new networks and bridges to accomplish the needed task. Physical therapy creates the **demand/directive, or need** for the brain to *find a new way* (among the 100 billion or so nerve cells) to accomplish the task that was previously performed by the damaged network of cells. As this new network is built, the person recovers. One of the most fascinating portions of the video is the actual capturing of the brain's neurons building a communication network.

Now, what I want to focus on is the *cause* of the construction of this information, communication, and action network. In the example of physical therapy, it is the repeated forcing of the body to perform certain tasks that cause the brain and nervous system to respond by building the network of connections that will make executing the task possible, easy, and ultimately automatic.

This is, no doubt, the exact way we develop from the womb to maturity. As we develop, the billions of neurons build the trillions of connections between each other to accomplish the goals of: function, growth, and maturity. Many of these connections are pre-programmed (innate), while others are created on-demand, out of specific individual needs as we interact with the world. In the *Discovery* video,[12] as a network is being built, you can see the dendrites reaching out/ growing in the direction of the new path.

Remember, before our brain prunes unneeded connections, there are many existing connections, like a tree with many branches, each a possible bridge to action.

What if no single, direct pathway is established between neurons, and every neuron that reached out to help were allowed to remain connected? The result would be many options for a task or the worst case would be something resembling confusion and instability, as the brain has no clear and

---

[12] http://alturl.com/4srut

certain pathway, but *many* possible paths or options, when only one is desired—the right one to produce proper function.

Illustration: Imagine a baseball team lost its ace pitcher (symbolic for essential neuron in a network) due to injury. The team needs to rebuild this network by finding the best replacement pitcher possible. The call goes out for try-outs. (These candidates are like the many dendrites reaching out as potential replacements in the network.). Once the best replacement for the injured pitcher is found the team will be complete once again. The closer the replacement pitcher is to the injured "Ace", the better the team's performance will be. (Likewise the better the repaired neural network in response to therapy, the closer the person will be to normal function.)

If the team takes its time deciding on a replacement, instability will continue. To establish new camaraderie and continuity with the new player, the team must cut unneeded candidates (like pruning unneeded neural connections), and decide on the one right pitcher to fill the gap caused by the injury. Not to mention the energy and resources consumed by all those unnecessary members of the network. One major reason for pruning is to make maximum resources and proficiency available for all the remaining members of the network—no waste and maximum production.

Can you imagine a state of vacillating between *this* possibility and *that* possibility? Should it be this path, or maybe that path? The implications are numbing! When we give our brains doubt and uncertainty, we are crippling the brains ability to create **one clear path** to the perfect performance or execution of a task.

Doubt is Tangible

A key observation which you may have already made, is that roadblocks like fear and doubt are not just psychological dynamics existing in the mind and imagination, but there is in fact a physical, tangible, biological aspect connected to these concepts.

"A double minded man is unstable in all of his ways"
—James

Notice the scripture quote implies the instability is not just in the mind (psyche) as in a mental problem. In other words, this instability or imbalance starts in the mind but affects "his ways," his paths. His thoughts are connected with his course of action, way of life. We are discovering there is a *real* biological affect which occurs on the cellular (neural) level, and determines the output and ultimate performance of the individual.

Lack of Confidence

If the brain were to build a *command, leading to action* network from mixed signals of uncertainty, the result would be confusion and instability. **Instead of a solid direct highway to your destination, envision a maze of intersecting and overlapping roads making it impossible to reach your destination in a timely manner. But, I am more inclined to believe the effects of doubt are most often inaction**—as the brain is not moved (by direct clear demand or need) to forge a specific pathway. Or a half-hearted effort at something you don't really believe in. **Doubt is a lack of confidence in the chosen path.**

I can't help but visualize the difficult performance of some task, due solely to the confusion caused by all of the possibilities—or rather impossibilities presented by doubt. **Doubt erects an obstacle on the bridge to accomplishment.**

∼

To understand more deeply the effect of doubt on the brain, and therefore performance, let's look at how the brain works from a different perspective.

The brain performs its tasks in two ways:

- The first is by necessity, which is programmed into the fiber by DNA. We don't have any conscious control in most of those tasks which the brain completes, making them automatic functions, such as walking or eating. We are only called in for conscious input if the need arises to learn them over again, thus re-establishing connections between neurons.

- The second way our brain performs its tasks includes the conscious input it receives through our senses: It does what we ask of it; For instance, if we are happy with an experience, our brain is certain to register the experience as pleasurable, and arrange for repeating the experience, because we have given a mental directive: "I like this," "This is good," "Remember this experience," "I would like to experience this again," etc.

The same happens with negative experiences, i.e. a warning will be recorded in our brain. An unpleasant experience will likely trigger a physical response later on when something associated with that experience re-appears. Phobias are an extreme example of this phenomenon, and some addictions are another example.

These conclusions can be confirmed by reflecting on our

development and maturing from birth. After birth we receive input from the world around us through our five senses. Our brain processes all of this information, and when the time comes, it begins to cause us to express ourselves through speech, emotions, behavior, and so forth, as we desire. We determine to express, and our brain takes on the tasks of accomplishing the desire.

Doubt (And Fear, for that matter) is a Verb

With this in mind, what are the possible results of doubt? **Since doubt is a verb and not an adjective, it is actually a directive or command from the mind. Doubt begs action.** This means the brain will receive doubt as a directive from your mind and will. You have responded to the situation and sent a directive to your mind like: "Whoa! I'm not sure about this." "Hold on, let's think about what to do." "Which way should I proceed?"

Unstable/Uncomfortable Ground

Doubt—although it is necessary in some situations to prevent error or warn of possible danger—acts as a dam or barrier in a river by stopping the smooth flow of information along the pathways to accomplishment.

  The brain is uncomfortable with indecision, because it is programmed to forge direct pathways toward goals, which will eventually lead to automatic and easy performance. How do I know the brain is uncomfortable with indecision? Because indecision is an *unstable state of being—a wavering, non restful state, and the uneasiness is in the mind.* Therefore we naturally seek relief from the unstable state of doubt by making a decision—often to retreat. (**When we retreat, we hope to return to the nearest place of stability and confidence. Many hopes have been abandoned by doubt.**)

Imagine sitting at a stop sign while the driver tries to decide whether to go straight, make a left or right hand turn, put the vehicle in reverse. As the minutes tick by, what are you as a passenger feeling? Frustration? Unease? The "safest" course of action would be to forget about going forward, and go back home. The same scenario can be used to illustrate how your brain responds as you vacillate.

A Certain Path to Doubt

We are in fact making it *impossible* to accomplish the goal because the only *clear* command is doubt. Some will say "well sometimes a good outcome will result even when I was unsure it would." That may be true, but that good outcome happened *in spite* of your indecision, not because of it. That would fall into the category of good fortune. That is—in my opinion—a dangerous way to live, because you are subject to anything but the best potential outcome. It is much easier and safer to be clear about the direction you want your brain to take you. This is what the brain is programmed to expect and respond to.

Doubt—Temporary Advisor

Although not as powerful as fear, doubt is *always* a hindrance to progress. If it is a rational application of the brakes, doubt should definitely be embraced, but only allowed a brief appearance—in other words, make up your mind quickly. **En-**

tertain as much doubt as you want during learning, training, planning, and practice, until the mind is made up, but
forbid it during performance.

In the event you still have doubts after your learning and
practice phase, you will have to lower your expectations, and
perform within the knowledge and skills you have mastered.
Go for what you know, not what you don't. Some endeavors
are too risky to attempt without proof you are capable of success. This reminds me of a TV commercial where this guy is
experiencing so much success and confidence in other areas
of his life, he is begging some guy juggling chain saws to toss
them his way. Let's be reasonable. Your future performances
will improve with training—as skills develop.

During most activities the penalty for entertaining doubt
would be loss of concentration, and a poor performance. In
dangerous or extreme sports, doubt could cost you your life,
as split second decisions are constantly made. In reaching toward other goals doubt will result in a late arrival. Let doubt
help only in the preparation stage.

**There is no way doubt can exist in The Zone, because
it is diametrically opposed to the positive free flowing cer-
tainty of The Zone Phenomenon, where actions appear to
leap from the eyes, ears, and hands, past the will toward
accomplishment...before you can even think. No Zone resident ever experienced the presence of doubt.**

When you think about it, the more *unconscious* control
the brain has, as in The Zone, the greater the precision of the
performance.

Double Minded

Double mindedness, as I see it, is different from doubt in that it is not as close to fear and uncertainty. It is simply the opposite of single mindedness. It is entertaining more than one immediate option, goal, or objective—essentially a dividing of confidence between both options.

It is similar to doubt in its ultimate effect on the brain, because it cannot produce a solid network of neurons along a single, optimal pathway toward accomplishing a goal. The key word here is *cannot*! **It is impossible for you as an individual, with certain strengths and weaknesses, to have more than one *optimal* way to accomplish a task; one is certain to be better than the other.**

Your job is to use your best judgment, based on knowledge, experience, and circumstances, to determine a *"give it my all" Plan A*. The Plan B or C will be held in reserve in the event that Plan A fails, or is no longer feasible.

Remember, the brain is designed to accomplish the tasks we set out to do, in the most efficient and proficient way possible, and when it does, to make it as easy and effortless as possible. It is not wise to ignore this fact and work against it by attempting more than one objective at a time.

Before I began to write this book, I came across an old article which I printed from the internet, about successful online businesses. Too bad I can't recall its author, but a bit of advice has stuck with me, and I want to share it. That advice goes something like this:

"Never pursue more than one business opportunity at a time. Only pursue more than one if the second helps

you to accomplish the first." —*paraphrased, Author unknown*

If what we know about how the brain forges new pathways is correct, this advice makes perfectly good sense. In the event a second, complimentary opportunity arises, the brain only has to *add to the current network* already in place, as opposed to starting from the beginning to forge a completely new pathway; or, (more time consuming, and laborious) forge two different pathways at the same time to accomplish two competing objectives.

My desire is to be self employed. If I attempt to start a graphic design business and a landscaping business at the same time, I can't possibly give each business 100%. On the other hand, if I add printing to my graphic design business, I have increased the potential of the design business instead of competing with it. The same is true in any other kind of endeavor.

Double mindedness can also be seen more vividly as split focus or focusing on two objectives at once.

Magicians understand this fact. We humans are not suited to dividing our focus. Your brain doesn't work that way. (pg. 110, *Keys to the City.*)

These principles also agree with the important, unalterable, law of specialization, which we'll analyze in chapter 9 (*Laws…*).

ALTERNATIVES TO FEAR AND DOUBT

It was suggested that Mohammad Ali didn't initially expect to beat the punishing George Foreman in the historic boxing match the *Rumble in the Jungle* in Zaire Africa.[13] Foreman's previous opponents didn't last long, because he was a powerful puncher. In fact, until then, he never had to go beyond two rounds. Foreman made quick work of "Smokin Joe Frazier" to gain the heavy weight title, which Frazier previously took from Ali. Now, Ali wants that belt back!

I'm not sure that fear is a good description of Ali's mindset before the match, but doubt was likely at some stage in his preparation process.

Fear and doubt can be a positive motivating force under certain circumstances (that boxing match being a case in point.) I believe it caused Ali to devise a way to conquer his formidable opponent. "Where there's a will there's a pathway."

In the planning stage, he devised the famous "rope a dope" strategy. It appears Ali plotted his options and prodded his opponent for weakness...finally resorting to a contender's best defense: **outsmarting your opponent.**

> *"It's not just athleticism that'll elevate your name,*
> *It's outsmarting your opponent,*
> *a think'n man's game"* —jw

There's no question Ali won that fight with his brain, by ingeniously detecting and exposing one—if not the only— weakness the *mighty* George Foreman had: pride and anger. Well, that's two.

First order of business was to survive the first two rounds. Then, Ali addressed his pride by taunting Foreman; who was not inclined to tolerate disrespect. No "sticks and stones may break my bones, but words will never hurt me" mentality. On

---

[13] http://un-conscious.com/videos/the-rumble-in-the-jungle

the contrary, this tactic exposed the other fatal fault in battle: anger! Foreman's anger caused him to lose all patience, throw caution to the wind, and unload all of his power reserves too soon in the battle.

The *"rope a dope"* was either brilliance or a successful, necessary survival strategy, or both. Either way, it proved victorious for the underdog, who employed it as brain power to make up for what he was lacking physically against his opponent.

Remember, our discussion on knowledge in chapter 4? Ali demonstrated the higher kind of knowledge, one which considers a thing from many angles which are not obvious to the average observer—as well as that subjects relationship to other things not normally associated with it. In this case, Ali *knew* the battle was not a contest of strength, athletics, or even speed and finesse (his forte), but one of psychology and wits. This is the "creativity" which comes with maturity, usually lacking in most young geniuses.

Knowledge and wisdom overcome fear and doubt. This is also a "key to the city."

Harnessed Fear

We return to the question: is fear *ever* a positive emotion *while playing* sports (or any other performance)? (I'm assuming Ali sorted his doubts out **before** he stepped into the ring.)

Well, it depends on at least one major consideration: is the fear rational?

Because our brain is programmed to send the entire body into fight or flight mode, releasing the powerful stress hormones into the blood stream, I believe fear induced adrenalin will have a negative, inhibiting, restrictive, affect, that is undesirable in most sports situations.

Extreme Sports is an example where we could understand fear from the athlete. However, the driving emotional force in the mind of the extremist is CONQUEST.

Because their fear is rational, it is utilized early in the processing, during learning, training, and developing their skills in the sport.

> *When you engage in extremes, fear is always a factor, but you keep it in check, it's the conquest you're after!* —J.W.

I remember, as a small kid, being fascinated (along with millions of spectators around the world) watching Evel Knievel (a professional daredevil)—arguably the father of modern day extreme sports—launch his motor cycle through the air over all kinds of obstacles, such as cars and buses.

> *"I fear dying but I can't quit because the banks won't let me."* —True "Evel" Quote

Although Evel acknowledged the presence of fear, he obviously harnessed it to make room for his many conquests.

Lack of Skill, Knowledge and Training:

Lack of skill (as an obstacle to The Zone) can be the result of being ill equipped (genetically) for the desired task, or failing to put in the required training to perfect a task. Listen...if I'm genetically meant to be 5' 8" tall, I can dream about being a center in the NBA all I want to, but the requirements for that goal are not in my possession.

Lack of knowledge and training are roadblocks which

rob the brain of tools it needs to construct highways for exceptional performance. It is impossible for performance to exceed potential, unless you are an acquired savant.[14] Although there are exceptions, it is safe to expect greater performance to follow greater knowledge and expertise. The more knowledge you possess...the more tools in your arsenal...the more soldiers in your army... the more players on your team. All of our learning and training institutions from pre-school to graduate school are designed to prevent these roadblocks. Learn, train, progress!

Head Games: Negative Affirmation/Distraction:

Rory McIlroy at the 2011 PGA Masters tournament is a good example of what the brain will do when you force it to focus on a *perceived* threat.

Here's what happened. The young Mr. McIlroy, a golf Phenom, was living up to expectations, and actually exceeding most experts and fans expectations after the first three days of the tournament. (Professional golf tournaments are played over four consecutive days.)

Out of the first 36 holes, there were only three holes he failed to par or better, and he had just missed par by one stroke on each of those holes. He was definitely in control of his game and the golf course. It was an impressive performance that raised the level of anticipation and excitement of everyone watching. He was leading the field of competitors by four strokes (a big lead) heading into the fourth and last 18 hole day.

---

[14] However, we'll consider whether or not the savant's great performance is miraculous or not, in the next three chapters.

On that last day when most top players were playing well, McIlroy, for no *obvious* reason, started off shaky: playing the first hole one stroke over par, and finishing that round of golf eight strokes over par. He finished the tournament tied for 15th place, to the astonishment of all.

McIlroy recovered very quickly from that disaster, (the likes of which claimed many professional athletes in the past who never recovered.) He went on to win the very next major tournament in a convincing fashion, and reached #1 in the world, and as of this writing, he is one of the 10 best golfers in the world.

But, what happened to him at the Masters? I believe like most observers that he experienced a mental breakdown. That is to say: the malfunction wasn't in his physical ability, it was in his head. To be more specific, it was in his mind— that faculty which gives directions to the brain about what we want and need to do.

I believe McIlroy focused on the obstacles and distractions at hand, which caused his brain to focus on them. This added to the number of commands the brain had to deal with, creating confusion as to what the brain should accomplish; and because some of the commands were negative, it naturally caused his brain to focus on a possible threat to his well being. A negative focus will receive more attention when set against positive thoughts (survival instinct).

McIlroy became tense, and hit many shots that were incredibly poor. He was obviously nervous—the paralyzing effects of unwanted stress hormones.

What your brain wants to hear from you is something like, "We've got 330 to the hole. A straight 200 yard shot with my favorite club will leave me 130 from the pin." The brain's response will be, "No problem...piece of cake...grab the club... take a few practice swings...and hit it about 200—we're sitting pretty."

This is so easy, that the brain will not even have to question the command, but will set into motion the execution, through pathways already established to produce that shot. After all, it didn't learn to play golf by negative "avoid this, don't do that" commands.

This is logical. We learn everything we have learned up to this point in our lives by *positively* applying the techniques and procedures required for each skill. Any negative corrective input is needed only in the learning and training stage. After we advance to become efficient and then proficient, the task becomes positively automatic with little if any *negative* input.

Because tasks and procedures involved in activities like golf require extremely complex coordination between the mind and body, it is understandable that the average person would need fine tuning, through positive reinforcement of skills already stored in memory, and correction of deviations, but not negative focus.

Rory had to learn this the hard way, and so do we.

Lack of Focus and Zone Extractions

Deutsche Bank Golf Championship 2012, Louis Oosthuizen opens with a birdie on the first hole...pars the second...enters The Zone on the 3rd hole playing alongside the hottest player of the year: Rory McIlroy. Oosthuizen continues to string birdie after birdie, for the next seven holes. That's seven birdies in a row, and eight birdies out of nine holes. You've heard this scenario at least twice already—Louis is on the path leading to golf's Holy Grail: 13 under par.

My friend, this Zone incident is a lesson in **what *not* to do when you are in The Zone.** "What are you saying" you ask? "He shot a course record 29 on the front nine, finished with the best round of the day (63), led the tournament by three strokes going into the final day, and you say he did something wrong?"

Well, either he did something wrong, or his playing partner/competitor (McIlroy) did something right. You see, had Oosthuizen continued in The Zone for just another two holes he would have been so far ahead that everyone else would have been battling for second or third place. Oosthuizen finished the tournament the next day one stroke behind the winner—Rory McIlroy.

I'm going to put the responsibility for this upset on McIlroy (smile), because I believe many competitors/performers don't have any idea how to stay in The Zone once they are there. I'm giving Oosthuizen a pass this time— but next time?

McIlroy, I'm assuming, after his monumental collapse the previous year, subsequent counseling and reflection, knew what The Zone felt like, looked like, and how *not* to make a premature exit. Realizing Oosthuizen was "in The Zone," McIlroy used a tactic I'll call an **"Emergency Zone Extraction."** This stealth weapon is designed to *awaken* The Zone resident out of his unconscious state, with a subtle yet harsh nudge back to reality!

I was astonished as I watched it unfold on that fateful day; "Is Rory deliberately using this tactic...does Louis know what is happening here...will it be affective?" I was asking myself. I would have to wait until the next few holes to know if McIlroy had used this deadly weapon effectively.

The Zone Extraction and How to Avoid It

The second nine holes in golf represent a psychological cross-road; either a chance to turn around a bad round or continue and finish a good front nine. If McIlroy was to deploy this invasive weapon, he would need to wait until the 10th hole to confirm Oosthuizen was indeed deep into The Zone, in which case extraction would be required. Louis started the back nine with another birdie on the 10th hole. A sense of urgency had to grip McIlroy as Oosthuizen rolled in that 20 feet birdie putt. Louis must be aroused out of his unconscious state..it's now or never!

This is how the maneuver was deployed: As Oosthuizen leaves the 10th green, McIlroy waits for him...moves in very close...they exchange words...laugh...and then...McIlroy bumps him with a shoulder—reminiscent of the chest bumps you see in other sports. Oosthuizen staggers a bit, laughs along, and they continue the conversation to the next hole. At that moment Oosthuizen is extracted back to normalcy, but he doesn't know it. Louis won't see another birdie until the last hole—but in the process made his first bogey (one over par) of the day.

Although it upset me to witness this extraction, McIlroy can't be villainized. He accepted a fact Oosthuizen failed to remember—they were in a competition, which had—I might add—a $600,000.00 difference between 1st and 2nd place.

In other sports "trash talk" is a well known and common

tactic used to distract and "get in the head" of opponents—especially if they are on a hot streak. For instance, the time-out call right before the critical punt in football, or free throw in basketball; injury time-out in tennis, etc. So, if McIlroy extracted Oosthuizen intentionally, it's fair play in competition.

As confirmation of my observations and assessment, I came across an article on foxsports.com which covered that day's action. McIlroy was quoted stating, *"I'm very happy that I'm still in 'touching' distance going into tomorrow."* He did enough literal "touching" to draw Oosthuizen's mind away from that *super natural* Zone of transcendent performance and back to the *tangible* world of normality.

Interestingly, the same article has Oosthuizen apologizing to McIlroy for having such a great streak, *"I told Rory, 'Sorry, but you've got to take it when you can.'"* (I wonder if this was just before he exited The Zone.) Did he mean *I'm sorry for playing better than you today. You deserve this more than I do; sorry for taking what is yours*? In total contrast, McIlroy took an aggressive, unapologetic: *I need this win* attitude. When Oosthuizen missed his birdie putt on 11, McIlroy made his birdie putt...waits around for Oosthuizen to finish, holds up a clinched fist, looks at him and asserts: *"I've got the honors"* and *"I feel like I've got a chance."* (More distraction to replace the calm mind of The Zone.) Oosthuizen is said to have high-fived and laughed along as they chummed it up to the next hole. I can guarantee that McIlroy wasn't chumming it up, but sported his "game face" while he was securing that trophy the next day.

Once a person assumes conscious, deliberate control

of their performance—diverting focus to peripheral matters—they have exited TZP of extraordinary performance.

Oosthuizen should have protected his complimentary
ticket into The Zone region like many great ones are known
to do. (Refusing to acknowledge distractions is the appropriate response to competitive extraction attempts.)

I shared earlier how Annika Sorenstam was given space
by her sister and caddy the day she shot 59 in The Zone. Baseball teammates always give the pitcher space when his got a
"no-hitter" going. It appears this "air is so rare:" out of respect
for the phenomenon those in close proximity allow it to flow
unhindered, even if that means your performance is mediocre
by comparison—The Zone truly is wonderful to behold.

Focus is *always* a good thing,—distraction *always* leads to
the exit.

In light of what we have previously discussed about the
power of 'NEED" to forge pathways for accomplishment, and
as a key ingredient for Zone access, it is just as reasonable to
have viewed this event from McIlroy's standpoint. He used a
powerful combination of his tenacious mind and skillful tactics to defeat a formidable competitor, and accomplish a goal,
much like Ali against Foreman.

Because this chapter is dedicated to obstacles, we needed
to view this event from the negative side. However there is
enough in this event for any who desire tactics for an "emergency extraction" of a competitor who is performing in The
Zone. **However, beware of those who would extract you
when you're hot!** A distraction attempt is not only seen between competitors when the prize can only go to the victor,
but is often used by those who "don't have a horse of their own

in the race", they simply don't want to see you reach your own goals. So, they may directly *throw* obstacles of negativity and discouragement your way, or *withhold* the encouragement every climber needs to reach the pinnacle.

TOO MUCH NEED: ANXIETY

One of the biggest problems for those who have experienced TZP, and understand the importance of need and focus, is needing it so much that it becomes a distraction. The person is thinking about maintaining a need. Mental coaches try to prevent this tendency by teaching: "stay in the moment," not overwhelming the brain, or weakening present performance by looking too far ahead. This is good advice, but there has to be some *forward*/future planning during performance. So, the question becomes how much forward thinking? **In TZP, this question is taken out of your hands as you are carried along on auto pilot.**

Assuming you are not in The Zone—instead of sweating over maintaining a strong need and focus, think about executing the *series* of tasks necessary for the goal: need + task 1, 2, 3 = goal!

Speed Bumps: Failure and Disappointment

It has been said that failure and disappointment are, to those who succeed, opportunities for learning. While to some, these *speed bumps* are occasions for discouragement and defeat.

The relationship between failure and success is well known to motivational speakers, who give examples from a large number of accomplished people who have experienced many failures before they finally "made it big."

I believe, understanding how the brain works transforms these anecdotes from theory into tangible fact. Remembering what we've learned about the brain's neural connections "pruning process", we can better understand the success of those who transcend, and overcome despite failure and disappointment along the way. If every new task or skill begins with a multitude of options—as a large number of connections between neurons—it is *necessary* that there be a *testing* of options until the *best pathway* is found. After the optimal, proficient, highway is identified, the unnecessary connections (failure) are allowed to break-off (prune) so as not to interfere in the future successful performance of the task.

This "testing" process must necessarily involve some "failure", or if expectations have been high, "disappointment." This is one reason why most highly successful individuals instinctively forge ahead through failure on their way to reaching their eventual goal.

KEY: So, the next time you meet the speed bumps of failure or disappointment along the road to The Zone, remember—your brain is in the testing and pruning phase.

CHAPTER EIGHT

Idols, Heroes, & Fanatics

"For who makes you to differ? And what do you have that you did not receive? And if you received it, why do you boast as if you did not receive?"
—Paul, Apostle

As the television cameras scan the sea of people, I saw a representation of every ethnic group in the country. Young and old, upper and lower classes, men, women, and children...there was excitement on every face, laughter, singing, cheering, even tears of joy on the faces of many. It was as though the whole nation was gathered to celebrate the election of its 44th president: Barack Obama. That evening, November 4, 2008, the overflow of emotions and passions were the culmination of years of expectations and hopes of many people who wholeheartedly believed a life changing event occurred in the election of their candidate—the candidate of "hope and change for the better."

The world is so hungry for someone to satisfy its strong desire to follow a leader, a winner. Well, that's putting it mildly; truth be told, we need someone to worship, or idolize—plain and simple.

Politics is not alone; the sports world embodies this mentality more than other entertainment industries, including Hollywood and the music industry. For some reason—which is hard to explain—many sports fans don't view their favorite sport as entertainment, recreation, or play. To them, there is always something meaningful to *prove* in every competition, and it can and does get personal.

To some extent, I believe this mentality exists because athletic performance lends itself so easily to comic book super hero type of physical exploits. Similarly, every hero or idol is elevated to super hero status by fans, whether it be through music, politics, acting, or science.

I can think of a few more explanations for this mindset. Perhaps it's because we feel a sense of ownership in the success of our heroes. We have a *personal* interest (investment and reward) in their success. We make this association through any personal connection we can make with them; for example, *our* national hero, "local hero does well," school *classmate* goes on to success, *my* candidate, etc. Even an indirect social connection (my cousin knows her sister etc.) or, any number of creative ways people use to identify with their idol. With this mindset, "their success is our success." "Get one for the team." "Bring the crown home." "We won;" etc.

The Down Side

The unfortunate consequence of this way of thinking is that the failure of the idol is perceived as our own personal failure. It's a letdown accompanied by all of the disappointment and loss of self esteem that comes with *genuine* personal failure.

I found an interesting blog post by Anthony Centore:

"The first time a client came into my office, explaining that he was depressed after his favorite hockey team had lost a championship game, I thought it was just a sarcastic exaggeration. But he was serious, and over the course of the hour, he explained his feelings of loss, despair, anger, and his inability to focus on his work.."[1]

I find this quote funny because Centore goes on to say the next day after sharing that incident his clinical supervisor admitted she too was depressed. I'm sure you personally know a "fanatic" or may even be one yourself.

The Seed of Fanaticism

A reason for this obsession may lie deep within us; stemming from an innate desire to prove *our* maximum potential; to conquer our domain; to push through to higher heights as human beings. If our heroes succeed, then mankind succeeds; Like adding another rung on the ladder that reaches continually upward. Conversely, the lack of progress means lack of hope, and stagnation—so we push our heroes to accomplish more.

(This prevalent frame of mind is one of the observations which triggered my interest in writing this book.)

When a *super* hero arises within any domain, the world takes notice. We all celebrate and embrace their accomplishments, even if we are not a fan of that area. How else does Mohammad Ali or Michael Jordan become famous all around the world? Marketing has something to do with it, but the world

[1] http://thriveworks.com/blog/sports-fan-depression-is-real-did-your-team-lose-last-night/

still has to buy what the marketers are selling...and they are certainly buying.

Did you see the news coverage of celebrations all over the world when Barack Obama won election in the U.S.? It appeared that the whole world felt some kind of very personal triumph in the victory of *their hero* after the political fight for the top position in U.S. government.

Historically in sports, and lately in politics, the disappointment is all too often mixed with resentment and bitterness—shown through attacks and passionate expressions of disapproval. Before the days of social media you would have to attend a sporting event to hear the things that diehard fans were saying to their hero who failed to live up to expectations. Today, a quick twitter search and you'd be shocked at the venom spewed at the once applauded idol. His or her failure no doubt inflicts deep *personal* hurt.

I was very shocked, when I searched Twitter for "Tiger Woods", to find quite a few bogus feeds, disparaging the golfer with all kinds of indecent insults and personal attacks. I said to myself: "It's a wonder he is able to focus, considering this kind of criticism and insult." For some reason he had, in the perception of some fans, so offended them, they believed he deserved their verbal venom, meant to strip him of all human dignity, and destroy his image in the eyes and estimation of others.

I hear and have seen reports from other parts of the world, which are 10 times as bad as here in the U.S. Such is our obsession with our idols and heroes.

A More Realistic View

There is another way to view our great athletes and performers, which I've already hinted at. I'm asking us to look at the big picture—the stage itself—and the individual contributions of great performers to their particular domains. Their exceptional performances confirm the worthiness of that endeavor as a past time, choice of entertainment, or test of human ability.

Most of all, I think the contribution of the great-ones should help satisfy our unconscious desire for human transcendence beyond the boundaries that currently exist. These boundaries are marked by records and statistics kept on past performances. For example, the upper limit of the total number of major league baseball home runs in a season (before Mark McGuire's 1998 season) was set by Roger Maris at 61. Sixty one home runs was a wall, that for 37 years no professional player could surmount. We were right to celebrate that conquest, it was a triumph of human ability…"we have indeed advanced over the previous 37 years".

Fanaticism

Contrast this perspective with an interesting historical commentary on Roger Maris' 1961 record breaking season, and the sad way it illustrates my previous point about idols and fanatics.

Baseball-almanac remembers that season:

"1961: The year a record was broken, hearts were broken, and a man's life was changed forever. Roger Maris will forever be known as the man that took Babe Ruth's record. The man that changed the record

> books. Maris was hated, booed, cussed, and generally
> abused by the press and fans for his chase of the most
> well-known mark in all of baseball: Babe Ruth's sixty
> single season home runs."

Instead of celebrating a triumph over boundaries, progress forward and upward, the fans of baseball mourned an ir-**rational** *personal* **defeat** at the hands of an *imagined enemy* (Maris). They fought hard to prevent it from happening. Go figure. It's worth visiting *baseball-almanic.com* to read the rest of their commentary on this sad story.

What About Progress

Don't we instinctively know we are capable of more? A move closer to perfection is not just the stuff of comic books or legend, right? After all, we've been told that we only use 20% of our brains. We also witness hints of possibility which are snuffed out by episodes of inconsistency. We witness streaks of mastery that inexplicably dissolve into apparent mediocrity, as the hailed Phenom comes up short of expectations. So we have reason to long for perfection or the *real* super hero.

When he/she does arise in our beloved sport or favorite past time, we should celebrate, and take a deep breath of relief, that our dreams of transcendence or perfection are still alive and well. The show will indeed go on—long live human exploits, and the greatness of our favorite past times to bring out the best in us!

The Babe (Ruth) gave us memories and set the bar so high, we thought it was all downhill from there. But, Maris gave us hope that the bar of human potential in the challenge of baseball can be raised even higher. **Hatred for the *new* potential** record setter is in essence an addiction to mediocrity, and a stand against mankind. Isn't it? Or is the need for selfish (my man, our team…) success too powerful a force to be overcome by a triumph for "All"?

THE POWER OF TIME

The law of time teaches us: that it has a say in when our abilities manifest, how long they can be enjoyed, and the quality of our talents, gifts, and performance. This law may also be referred to as the law of diminishing ability, the law of life cycle, the law of erosion, or any number of descriptions for the fact that age has a powerful, absolute affect on all human ability and potential.

Under this law, youth is the optimal window for physical performance, while adulthood is the time-frame for optimal intellectual and emotional performance (which grows through experience).

Age will cripple physical ability, and may also weaken mental and emotional performance. Even though we are able, through good eating and exercise, to lengthen the days of physical strength, and keep a sharp mind for even longer, we can't— on this planet—defeat the Law of Time, Period.

Understanding this law helps us in the planning stages of our life, and helps us to form realistic expectations: Obviously, if physical talents manifest themselves in my youth, I would be wise to cultivate that talent then. On the flip side, it's not wise to expect a child to possess adult level mental and emotional maturity…give them time to develop those areas of ability. Scripture say's: *"It's not wise to put a novice in a leadership position,"* due to lack of seasoning required of leaders.

Professional athletes routinely prepare for short careers, out of respect for The Law of Time; knowing it will erode their physical abilities, and eventually rendering them unable to compete against younger opponents.

One positive aspect of this Law is that you're not finished when your physical abilities diminish as you approach mid-life. Fortunately, your brain cells are some of the last to go, and are capable of learning new experiences, lessons, and wisdom throughout your life. So performance potential in intellectual areas can grow, or at least maintain a high level, as the Law of Time exerts its powerful influence on my life.

Out of respect for the powerful *Law of Time and diminishing ability*, most people are instinctively led to religious pursuits in hope of an afterlife and continuation of consciousness...that's another journey.

The Big Picture:

What does this have to do with Idols Heroes and Fanatics?

If we look at our heroes and idols in a broader perspective, instead of a narrow laser-like focus on them, the anxiety and frustration that comes with unrealistic expectations will disappear. The games, music, entertainment, and politics will continue long after our heroes fade; After all, the window of peak performance closes pretty quickly after the athlete reaches their mid-20's—in most sports. Although the mind may remain sharp, (knowledge and skills increase with experience), the body is losing strength and flexibility as we pass our peak, somewhere around 35 years old.

We understand this and send our strongest to the battlefield in times of war. Biologically we transition from children to puberty or adulthood (able to reproduce our own children) somewhere around the age 12. This tells me we are at our reproductive strongest (able to produce seeds—a sign of mature growth) early in life rather than later.

As for the brain, by the time our hero reaches the age at which we have recognized his/her potential to occupy the throne, around the mid-20's, the body has reached its peak development. Granted, there is a brief plateau before the slow downhill turn. Nevertheless, the glory is beginning to slowly but surely fade. We would love to enjoy their heroics for decades but, to use southern vernacular, "that ain't gonna happen."

Most exceptional athletes demonstrate a prodigious ability in their chosen sport very early in childhood. There is a young 15 year old girl, Lydia Ko, tearing up the ladies professional golf association tour. She is sure to become a force as she matures physically and experientially. She is following the pattern of all truly gifted performers. On the PGA a 19 year old named Jordan Spieth has claimed a place among the best in the world—he's on schedule for greatness. There are too many others to mention. No doubt you can name several such examples without much thought.

With that in mind, it is easy to understand how 10 or so more years of experience and training produce a perfecting of those skills, as the physical body has matured at the same time. Finally, with experience, the strength of muscular development and solid brain networks, our hero emerges in all the glory of physical superiority. But the flower that reaches full bloom must subsequently fade.

One Hit Wonders

It also takes time to know whether or not that great performer is a "one hit wonder," operating under a brief period of inspiration or is being influenced by a *temporary* Zone residency. We have seen many apparent idols and heroes turn out to be one hit wonders. So, exercise patience; and count your chickens after they hatch, not before.

The Moral of This Story

Our *expectations* for our heroes should be realistic, and our *demands* on them should be realistic. They unfortunately cannot live up to unrealistic expectations...they are only human.

CHAPTER NINE

The Laws Of The Land

*"A wise man will hear, and will increase learning; and a
man of understanding shall attain unto wise counsels:"*
-Proverbs 1:5

When it comes to the idea of greatness, are there the haves
and the have-nots, as some suggest, and others fear? Are
those incidents we often witness of extraordinary, transcendent, super human feats, a peak into man's latent potential? Are we all welcome into that Zone of Transcendence, or
is it reserved for the privileged few?

Few among us reach a level of sustained transcendent performance. And of those who do experience the phenomenon,
most experience it for brief periods of time. And many never
experience it at all in their lifetime. It is reasonable to suspect
some kind of inequality in who are selected (allowed access)
into this region. Inequality in the genetic distribution of gifts,
talents, and assets, such as height and physical strength, is an
undisputed fact of life. This perceived discrimination is the
basis of the fear of some: that no matter how hard they would
try, they have, through no fault of their own, been excluded
from this desirable territory of super human performance. I

have heard people say for example: the child prodigy "makes me feel dumb".

If the idea of "latent" super human potential (within us all) is true, any demoralizing thoughts could be replaced by a hope of tapping into that potential. This chapter is written to analyze the laws governing The Zone (some of which have already been touched on), with a view to determining how they apply to all its residents, and if they favor some, and unfairly prohibit others.

LAW #1: BENEFICIUM

The term "law" is often used to refer to universal principles which describe the fundamental nature of something—universal properties.[1] This first law of The Zone governs everything, not only in The Zone territory of transcendence, but in every other region of our world. **Wherever we go on planet earth, there runs a distinctive thread of involuntary privilege.** No amount of scientific theory can erase the candid observation that the world itself, including and especially The Zone, is an involuntary phenomenon. Hence, The Zone is essentially an *un-conscious* state; **every single resident acknowledges this fact.** Why is this important you ask? Because, every other law springs out of this all encompassing one.

With any attempt to unlock the mysteries of transcendent human performance, we must not deny the reality of *involuntary* inspiration, or escalation of individual potential. A failure to see or a decision to ignore this most glaring aspect of human transcendence, is to begin the quest for meaning on the wrong path. On the other hand, to recognize the obvious

---

[1] en.m.wikipedia.org/wiki/Law_(principle)

presence of the involuntary nature of this phenomenon is to approach the phenomenon face to face, on its own terms.

A state of unconsciousness is the thread which runs through this book. It is the least common denominator of EVERY experience witnessed and shared involving The Zone.

This book is also guided by another principle: "give credit where it is due." A wise man (crediting inspiration), commenting on human ability once wrote:

> "What do you have that you didn't receive? If you did receive it, why do you boast as though you didn't receive it?"[2]

There is very little in this life for which the individual can take full credit. From, to whom we were born, to our immune system that keeps up alive, to our physical and mental attributes and capabilities; there is little for which we can claim personal credit. This fact is unsettling to some, who see it as a blow to autonomy, self esteem and ambition..."If something else is responsible for my successes", where's *my* esteem." "If the deck is stacked against me, why try"?

I see things differently. I have come to believe that knowledge of the *truth* is far more encouraging to self esteem than to discover that I have been operating under self delusion. Even worse, to be discovered by others to have taken credit for something I'm not responsible for. How many times have you heard someone in desperation admit this truth while exclaiming: "I didn't ask to be born."..."I wish I had other parents."..."If I had her talent," etc.

---

[2] Apostle Paul, first letter to Corinthians

I guess a need to know "why me, or why them and not me" (a rational inquiry) is the cause of discontent on all sides.

I've even observed a number of very wealthy people experience a strong sense of guilt and responsibility on account of their *undeserved* fortune.

If we accept this principle of involuntary access to the privileged region of The Zone Phenomenon, then we must approach this phenomenon on its terms not ours. As *essentially* passive participants and spectators, we must take what it (TZP) gives us, what it teaches…then learn and be enriched.

We have already looked at a few effects of ignoring this principle in the last chapter on *Idols, Heroes, and* Fanatics.

LAWS #2 & 3: DIVERSITY AND SPECIALIZATION

Michael Jordan may have been an exceptional basketball player, but he proved to be a not so good baseball player; and I hear, about the same at golf. The set of skills needed to be a successful, spectacular baseball or golf player are not present in Jordan's repertoire of skills.

It's a bit of a puzzle to some, that exceptional talent is usually restricted to a specific area of performance. As a fact of history, many of the greatest achievers to have made valuable contributions to our world have been failures (in comparison to their talents) in other areas of their lives and endeavors.

Very few have demonstrated exceptional abilities across several disciplines. One notable exception would be Michelangelo the great painter and inventor, who appeared to have a high level of understanding and ability in many areas. I'm sure there are other exceptions, but *the rule* is a narrow area of exceptional talent.

We are so inclined to expect a single exceptional gift to indicate overall greatness, that a successful athlete or entertainer can instantly become a leader to millions...a political candidate with clout...a business consultant to fortune 500 companies...and a role model for the children of the world. We expect greatness to envelop everything the person does—"they are chosen." Unfortunately, this common inclination contradicts the powerful laws of diversity and specialization.

Diversity means being different and unlike other things or persons, and includes the idea of being unique. Closely connected to the principle of diversity is the law of **specialization**, which means, not only are we different, but we, along with all other organisms, have specialized abilities, talents, and functions.

These two interconnected principles characterize and govern the relationship of every cell to the living organism. The fact that each individual brain cell is diverse from all others, highlights the law of diversity. The fact that each cell is *designed and programmed* to be different, indicates its diversity is *intentional*, and therefore, it has a specialized (unique) function and purpose.

These principles apply to each of us, as well as our gifts, talents, and abilities. Because these laws are closely connected, we will consider them together.

Embrace Your Uniqueness

I believe, based on these principles, we should embrace our individual diversity, and not seek to be someone else. We should realize that we are born with some specialized ability and seek to find that ability/abilities, embrace, and then maximize our potential. The inclination to use the success of others as an **exact** pattern for our own ambitions is misleading.

I don't believe a scientific study is necessary to validate the existence of these principles, because they are such an integral part of our world, their existence may be ignored but not denied.

Well, I take that back...at times men are known to deny the reality of things everyone else with eyesight clearly sees. The rationale for denying the idea of individual talent, leans on *interpretation* of the evidence: Although diversity is clearly seen, the interpretation of this reality may go something like, "the reason there are managers and workers, is because the workers are less ambitious and or intelligent. All are meant to be managers; that level of function is the intended goal of every worker, some just fail to reach that goal. Everyone is dealt the same hand; it's just how you play it."

To which I ask: If all were *driven* to be managers, how much work would get done in an organization? That organization is certain to collapse if it ever gets off the ground. Every cell can't be a glorious brain cell can it?

Just as we all have unique fingerprints, we are all unique in our contributions to the world. No matter how much you may attempt to transform yourself into your favorite idol, **it can never happen.**

To fight against this law, in the pursuit of trying to be someone else, is not only futile but irrational.

Conceit

Equally irrational is to think arrogantly of your individual abilities, compared to others. Like a football quarterback feeling superior to the rest of the team. Can he compete by himself? If you are so important and everyone else if dispensable, remove the waste management companies from your world, and see how long you last. Your world would very quickly become one in which, not you, but disease reigns king.

It is important to stress these two laws, not only to help us pursue the path where our strengths lie (increasing our potential for success), but to prevent us from looking down on others (from our "higher level" of accomplishment,) who are "lower" on the ladder of achievement, and therefore value. These laws teach that you are certainly different, but not better or more important than others. Not only are the "higher ups' unwilling to do the work of the "lowly," but are likely *not able* to do it with the same proficiency. Have you ever seen the TV show *Undercover Boss —it teaches this lesson every episode*? Hardly any of the executives from the corporate offices are able to do the work of the employees on the front lines. In fact, on a recent episode the undercover CEO was fired by his employee because of incompetence—he was a pathetically slow learner, so he had to be fired. So, let these laws teach us to think of ourselves, others, and our heroes rationally.

Diversity and Twins

Even identical twins, with the same DNA, are unique in many ways, such as personality, temperament, talents, and interests.

A 2008 article in SCIENTIFIC AMERICAN™ written by

Anne Casselman,[3] referencing a number of experts in the field of twin studies and genetics, concludes that identical twins are different at the genetic level. It appears that having shared the same single egg at conception, and the same physical appearance, they are otherwise very different. This is very interesting, considering identical twins are "made" at the very same moment, out of identical material, same sperm cell and same egg cell. Yet, they are two different products. **If any two people *could* be the same, identical twins would be, but they are not.**

It is also observed that the brain's cerebellum region is as different between identical twins as it is between any two people. The cerebellum is recognized as the brain's center for coordination and other motor functions, but it is also involved in cognitive functions like language, emotions, and attention.[4] It is also true according to the experts, and observation, that they grow more different as time goes by, due to different life experience. It appears that no two individuals develop in exactly the same way, even if they share the same birth event.

Our understanding of genetics and reproduction, indicate that many traits of our species (human) are carefully protected during reproduction so that we reproduce humans. These traits are physical and biological but soul level differences are allowed, so that we maintain individuality. So identical twins can have indistinguishable physical differences, but completely different souls, even though the same exact material produced them.

No two people are the same or can be the same; therefore,

---

[3] http://www.scientificamerican.com/article.cfm?id=identical-twins-genes-are-not-identical
[4] http://en.wikipedia.org/wiki/Cerebellum

diversity is a natural law in our world including The Zone. Expectations, attitudes, and efforts, should be adjusted accordingly.

THE WORLD AND DIVERSITY

These truths are also apparent from mere observation of the world around us. I consider these truths indisputable. We may debate how and why, but not the reality of diversity and specialization.

Let me offer even more powerful proof.

Every single cell in our body has a specialized function, which when performed properly, makes a vital contribution to a healthy productive human being, able to accomplish tasks and enjoy the pleasures of life. If hair cells attempted to be eye cells, we would be in trouble. But when all cells function as designed...all is well.

In a much broader perspective, if all birds were eagles we would know nothing of the song bird, the bat, the delicious barbecue chicken, or deep fried turkey:-) If all sea life were gold fish, Sea World would not exist. If all flowers were roses, to what would we compare their beauty? If all clovers were three leaves, there would be no Saint Patrick's Day. You get the point; diversity is a good thing. Let's embrace it!

INNATE SPECIALIZATION

Thank God our world is so diverse and wonderful—and the unintelligent (non-human), from the one celled amoeba, to the killer whale, to the scavenger vulture, have no choice but to embrace their diversity, and live out their specialized function; Thereby contributing essential balance, harmony, and beauty to the world. It is only we humans with a much higher level of intellect, volition, and brain power, who are often determined to be what we are not suited to be, particularly, someone else.

Whenever the topic of success in any area of life is discussed or contemplated, the question of a repeatable pattern always arises. "You can repeat his/her success!" Can you indeed "be like Mike?" There are a plethora of how-to books (you may have grabbed this one for the same reason) touting a secret to repeating the successes of other exceptional human beings. Based on the sales of these type of books, it is a good bet that most of us believe, or at least hold out a hope, that we can indeed "be like Mike," "be Tiger Woods," achieve like Bill Gates or Steve Jobs, or even look like a super model.

The facts indicate that *it is possible* for *everyone* to reach a level of outstanding, even Zone-like success in their life—the *potential* is there, and the raw material is present in all of us. The difference lies in the diverse and specialized way that raw material is programmed to manifest in each of us, and whether or not we discover it. That's what this book is all about.

LAW #4: RESPECT THE POWER OF THE LAW

This fourth law may sound like an attempt at being clever, but I believe it's necessary to add this principle as a law because it is often overlooked or ignored. To put this law succinctly, if your area of expertise or endeavor is well established and has identifiable laws governing its performance...make sure you know them.

Keeping in mind the first three universal laws which govern how *all things* work and relate to each other. Ignoring the first (Beneficium) will result in a distorted perception of the talents you possess, especially their value compared to everyone else. Ignorance of the next two, diversity and specialization, will result in wasted energy and effort by trying to emulate someone else, misplaced expectations, and ignoring or under-developing your own natural abilities.

After understanding and embracing the first three laws, we can turn our attention to the special laws affecting any particular area of performance. The more you know about those laws, the stronger foundation you will be able to build upon, while pursuing a goal of exceptional performance.

Law #4 is about the necessity of being a good student. Knowledge or learning is a fundamental part of everything we *do* in this life. Every system of education is built upon it—from pre-school to post graduate school. The relationship between knowledge and performance is universally accepted. Some of its principles are:

- The more you know, the greater your performance potential.

- Knowledge must begin with the fundamentals/foundation, then built upward.

- The fundamental laws governing an area of performance never change, but may be forgotten...It will be necessary at times, to confirm the foundation is intact.

Sean Foley, the golf instructor, who came to notoriety after becoming Tiger Woods' third instructor since turning professional, is known for his scientific approach to teaching professional golfers how to improve their games. He appeared on a

Golf Channel instruction segment, and sounded more scientific then any instructor I've ever heard—I was impressed as well as enlightened.

Foley has been harshly criticized by some golf commentators and analysts for going away from playing the game by "feel" or "instinct," and relying too much on the cold mechanics of "machine-like" physics in his teaching methods.

One of the approaches used in this book to teach the "secrets of The Zone," follows the same general philosophy. Starting with the most essential, the "least common denominator", which needs to function properly for the whole system to function properly, and then take care of every other component in the process toward optimal performance. This is an approached based on logic, physics, and biology. If that cell can't function properly, the entire system is subject to malfunction. This approach can also be understood as going from "cause to effect"..."Let's understand what causes this action to happen."

Golf happens to be a game I've acquired a passion for, so pardon my returning there for illustrations. However, there are lessons here that apply anywhere.

Although many experts and critics (many, former professional golfers themselves) believed it would be impossible for Tiger to return to the top of the professional tour, I believed otherwise, based largely upon what we are about to study in the next chapter: genetics, gifts, and talents, all of which are a law by themselves. The other factor causing me to doubt the opinions of some "experts", was my belief that anytime a performer is running into trouble performing their craft, and decides to return to the foundation, and make sure it is solid, they are doing the right thing. This is a foundation-up philosophy, a "make sure the 'cause' is present and the 'effect' will follow" philosophy. Foley rebuilt Tiger's swing based partially on the physics of how *every* golfer hits good shots—those laws which have to be adhered to hit a good shots. This is an example of #4 *Respect the Power of The Law's*—of golf.

In full agreement with the principle we've learned, that teaches: the brain seeks the most efficient path for accomplishing every task, so as to eventually make it easy and automatic, (unconscious), Foley helped Tiger reduce the number of movements in his golf swing, simplifying the task, and lessening strain on his body, effectively extending his golf career. That's called acknowledging the laws of age/deterioration, and planning accordingly. **A principle here is: know the fundamental laws governing your area of performance, and respect them.**

Now let's move on to another law of The Zone that deserves its own chapter: *Heredity*, which will enhance and complete what may be lacking in the other laws.

CHAPTER TEN

The Law of Heredity

"The apple doesn't fall far from the tree"

T he passing on of traits from parents to their offspring is a law affecting performance in and out of The Zone.

Inside the Zone: Although extraordinary performance is not likely to run in families, sometimes it does. Additionally, the potential for exceptional performance has to be contained within the DNA of the species for it to surface in the first place. Therefore, even if transcendent performance can't be obviously linked to a parent, it was nonetheless transmitted through the parents. The only exception would be a miracle, such as a man walking on water; even then, Jesus attributed that ability to his father[1].

Outside The Zone: Inherited traits or characteristics among close family members are much more obvious. The debatable parts are: which characteristics, how much of a trait can be inherited, and how much is learned from environmental influence? This is the long standing nature versus nurture debate.

I will tell you up front: logic tells me all performance po-

[1] The Gospel of John, chapter 10

tential is inherited through our parents, because in their seed (the nature side of the debate,) the creative (building, manu-facturing) process takes place, as we are conceived, and grow to adulthood and full potential. Experience (nurture) doesn't "create" anything, it just uncovers or draws out the potential that resides within us. In that sense, everything we accomplish had its seed in heredity, which was passed on to us from our parents.

In this chapter we'll try to understand this law, the role it plays in our lives, and how this powerful law influences our individual abilities, talents, gifts (even temperaments), and therefore, our potential. We'll also consider how to find your area of talent for optimal performance—if you don't already know it.

Let's begin this look into the role of genes and heredity on our talents, abilities, and performance potential, by starting not with the genes themselves, but the parts which compose them. This chapter is an enhancement to the last chapter, and complement to chapter three, *The Power Source*, because it relies on science to enhance our appreciation of TZP in par-ticular and the phenomena of life in general.

THE ATOM

The smallest part of all matter that can-not be broken down by ordinary chemical means is called an atom. As a unit com-prised of protons, neutrons, and electrons, the atom is the least common denomina-tor of all things tangible (physical, material).

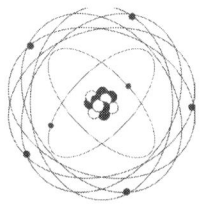

Atom

We're not even going into "sub-atomic" particles; it's beyond our purpose.

Their Size: Atoms have to be magnified *45 million* times their normal size to be seen under a microscope. Even at that size the individual parts are still not recognizable—they appear as one solid object. A drop of water has more than a million, million, billion atoms.

Their Power: The part I find most fascinating is: In the core of our body, the smallest particles are active, moving entities endued with energy and power. Electrons zoom in orbit around the nucleus. This tells me that a certain amount of power and potential lie at the core of who we are. **This makes it less incredible a thing to observe a product composed of such power and energy exhibiting phenomenal performance. Phenomena is what we're made of.**

In mankind, atoms come together and contribute to the greatest performance potential known on earth. When we examine the individual parts which make up any form of life on earth, and compare them with what we are able to produce with our superior intellect, we should be astonished at the incredible precision and productivity of these miniaturized wonders.

The DNA Molecule:

Two or more atoms chemically connected or bonded together form a molecule. DNA is a large molecule made up of many smaller molecules. One type of molecule that makes up the DNA molecule is called a base.

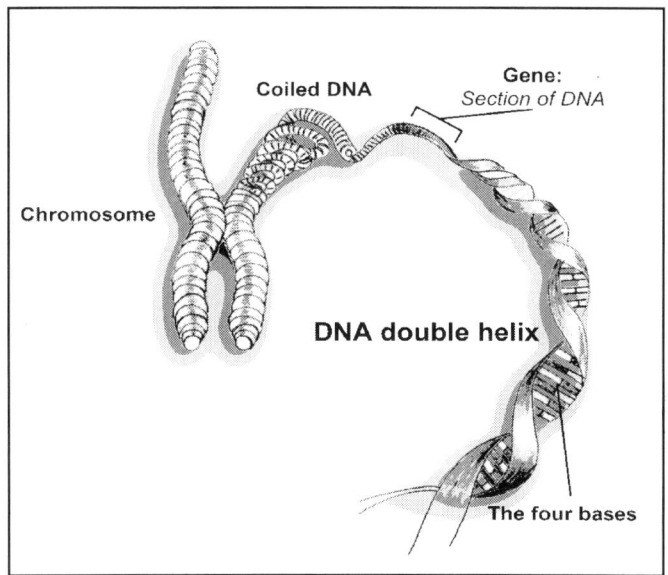

Coiled DNA

Gene:
Section of DNA

Chromosome

DNA double helix

The four bases

DNA Molecule and some of its parts.

Bases

The *three billion* bases (the building blocks of the DNA strand), have been compared to letters, whose arrangements form words, and the combination of these words form sentences with meaning, in a special, complex language—the language of life. Those tiny energized atoms have come together to produce the phenomenal DNA language of life.

> *"It would take about 9.5 years to read out loud (without stopping) the 3 billion bases in a person's genome sequence. This is calculated on a reading rate of 10 bases per second,"*[2]

---

[2] http://news.sciencemag.org/sciencenow/2012/09/human-genome-is-much-more-than-j.html

In 9 months this information produces human life. The amazement continues.

I am not writing this so that you will understand all this stuff—although some of you will. My intension is to show the potential inherent in the human body, based on the phenomenal assembly and contribution of parts, and the history of the incredible performance of those parts, beginning at our conception. The incredibly intelligent programmed *language*, letters (bases), words (the rungs of the ladder,) communication (the arrangement of the words into sentences,) and meaning (instructions interpreted and executed,) of the DNA code shouldn't be overlooked either, as we consider our potential.

A. E. Wilder-Smith compares the DNA to a scroll of information that reads and executes its own instructions:

> *It resembles, that is, a hypothetical architect's plan of a house, which plan not only contains the information on how to build the house, but which can, when thrown into the garden, build entirely of its own initiative the house all on its own without the need for contractors or any other outside building agents...Thus, it is fair to say that the technology exhibited by the genetic code is orders of magnitude higher than any technology man has, until now, developed.*[3]

Professor Gitt reminds us that this **book** of self-executing information is equal to 15 million, million, pocket sized paperback books (160 pages each); enough for 6 billion people to get 2,500 copies each.[4]

This is the substance of human potential and it is intel-

---

[3] Wilder-Smith, A.E. (1987), *The Scientific Alternative to Neo-Darwinian Evolutionary Theory* (Costa Mesa, CA: TWFT Publishers).
[4] Werner Gitt, *The Wonder of Man (1999)by CLV · Christliche Literatur-Verbreitung*

ligent, energized, powerful, and effective in its purpose—it produces phenomenal life—over and over again.

Now, how is it transmitted from parents to children?

How Heredity Begins

When it comes time for the body to prepare reproductive (egg and sperm) cells, the DNA inside of that cell packages itself like stuffing a suitcase for a trip: The DNA which normally floats loose inside the nucleus of a cell, begins to wind itself into tighter and tighter coils, until it becomes capsule-like structures known as **chromosomes** (refer to previous diagram). Just a reminder: you cannot see a human cell with your naked eye—not to mention the nucleus where all of this is taking place. Cells are much smaller than the period at the end of this sentence; the nucleus occupies only 10% of that space.

Each human reproductive cell—the transporters of hereditary information—contains 23 of these compact DNA capsules, which together comprise *nearly* all of the information (those three billion bases) required to manufacture a human being. I say *nearly,* because the rest of the necessary information and material come from other parts of the cell, which are copied and transported also,[5] together with a matching package from the other parent.

When the egg and sperm cells (with their DNA payloads) combine, the miracle of reproductive life and heredity commence. To appreciate just how powerful a law heredity is, and to refresh or improve our knowledge, let's examine more of the players in this drama.

---

[5] Page 29 shows a single brain cell and its many parts.

GENES

Genes are particular sections along the DNA molecule. They are the words and sentences produced by the letters (bases). Our genes contain construction plans. *"There, in code, we find instructions about how our eyes, ears or heart and all the physiological details of our bodies are formed, as well as all our abilities."*[6] Experts say, around 21,000 genes are distributed among the 23 chromosomes received from one parent.

Genes' system of instructions is very complicated, because genes can overlap, and have multiple beginnings and ends.[7] A U.S.-funded project, called the Encyclopedia of DNA Elements (ENCODE), uncovered *four million* spots in our DNA which act as switches controlling gene activity. Those switches can be both near and far from the gene they regulate, and act in different combinations in different cell types to give each cell type a unique genomic identity."[8] That is, the exact same switch serves a different function, with a different set of partners in an eye cell then it does in a brain cell. I find this on the amazing side! Don't think anyone understands this completely—no one does, but we're learning every day.

Until the **2012** ENCODE project, scientists didn't know that genes overlap each other, or that several—perhaps many—switches work together on a single gene, from different locations along the DNA molecule. This adds serious complexity to heredity which we are still learning about. I want us to realize that the ***automatic*** functions of our body

---

[6] Warner Gitt, *The Wonder of Man*
[7] http://news.sciencemag.org/sciencenow/2012/09/human-genome-is-much-more-than-j.html
[8] Ibid

are extremely sophisticated, and flawlessly executed. So much so we take it for granted.

We are very likely to discover in the future that some information is accessed from all genes at the same time, for a single purpose, in the same way all of our senses work together. We've seen that in The Zone Phenomenon; all of the senses become engaged together: the eyes see the scene, hearing is narrowed to critical sounds, while everything else is muffled; sense of touch becomes fine tuned as the body responds with precision to what the mind needs to accomplish. As a matter of fact, we know if adrenaline comes in to play it has an effect on the entire body. This can only occur if all of the individual cells respond in harmony. The synchronicity and collaboration of DNA information accessed and executed within the cells, has to resemble a one trillion member orchestra, as all cells respond to *one* need, and work in concert to accomplish it. If this is the case, scientists would have to examine a very large number of genes in a very large number of cells at the same time to map the sequence of genes involved in a single function.

Heredity and Diversity

All genetic blueprint information is inherited in pairs—half from the father and half from the mother. Additionally, characteristics from one parent include a mixture of genetic information from their father and mother. For example, if the genes defining your eye color came from your mother, they likely are a combination of traits from both her parents, thereby ensuring genetic diversity—**each of us is a unique human**

**being comprised of characteristics from all of our ances-
tors.**

Diversity is also certain because many genes are very sus-
ceptible to **"crossover"** when the complimentary chromosomes of Mom and Dad pair up—which is done differently
every time—and is most likely controlled by those "switches"
we talked about.

> *"By recombination I mean crossing-over, insertions,
> deletions, transpositions, jumping genes, and any other
> enzyme mediated process. Since re-combinations
> are enzyme-mediated, it reasonably implies that God
> created recombination to be the primary means of
> variation..."[9]*

Mr. Williams attributes recombination (the cause of individual differences) to "God's" design, because it is caused
by enzymes aiding the process, which indicate an intelligent,
cooperative (not random) process. This "recombination" is a
type of unique information transfer between identical genes
from each parent, resulting in different characteristics in each
of their children. The enzymes which mediate this process receive their instructions from genes. The genes are conductors
in the concert played by the enzymes.

Because recombination occurs each time chromosomes
combine, you are therefore more or less a product of the blueprints used to construct all of your ancestors including your
two parents. **Your performance potential** as a human being
comes out of this inheritance.

I don't know how you are receiving this information, but I
don't get the picture of a blank slate upon which our environ-

---

[9] Inheritance of biological information—part III: control of information
transfer and change by Alex Williams

ment writes and produces whatever it unintentionally pleases. But I'm getting ahead of myself.

Picture genes as thousands of volumes of a single encyclopedia set. Each volume contains blueprints and instructions for building, repairing, maintaining and duplicating a part of that human being. Each volume would also be intricately linked with all other volumes so as to execute one central purpose—maximum potential for the person in which it resides.

THE CASE FOR HEREDITARY TALENTS

There are many scientists, philosophers, and theorists, who don't believe in the idea of talents or gifts. I believe most of them disbelieve because, the idea seems "unfair"; it implies a type of discrimination among men—creating "haves and have-nots." Instead, they believe all men begin with the same blank slate—it's then up to the individual what he writes on that slate. No one has a genetic (talent) advantage in any area of life. All success and failure can be traced to environmental factors such as socioeconomic influences, luck, education, training, etc. Instead of the "haves and have-nots" it's the "do and do-nots." The do's are to be identified and celebrated for their high achievements, whereas the do-not's are to be pitied as underachievers. (The amount of status and wealth usually distinguish the two.)

As additional validation for the belief in innate talents and abilities, we only need to talk with the parents, teachers, trainers, recruiters, and coaches of the world, who are forced to recognize differences in ability among people. As a result, they structure education around those differences. One logical reason for any distinctions and special attention in our educational system, is so that those with advanced development in certain areas might not have their development hindered by an inadequate level of teaching and training. And the less skilled may be more slowly developed. Additionally, to identify particular skills among all students and train them accordingly.

Sports teams rely on Scout's ability to recognize talent, as a means to assembling a winning team. Sports trainers and talent scouts will tell you that "God given talent" is a premium when it comes to the ability to compete and excel.

THE POWER OF HEREDITY

Many basic facts about heredity can be known by mere observation, without the assistance for scientific experiment and analysis. For example, we human beings are more alike than we are different—whether we are from Europe, Africa, Asia, etc. **All human beings differ in genetic make-up by only 0.01 percent. Or putting it positively: all human beings are genetically 99.99 percent identical.** So then, what are we fighting for? Surely we can find an enemy that is not so much like ourselves. (I digress.) Therefore *"Almost all human genetic variation is relatively insignificant biologically."*[10]

This tells us that **heredity is a mighty powerful law** with powerful controls: humans have reproduced humans with many common characteristics, but few variations, and that, in superficial (mostly visible) characteristics. (This system of reproduction and heredity has continued across the world with exacting accuracy, for as long as we can empirically ac-

---

[10] http://science.education.nih.gov/supplements/nih1/genetic/guide/genetic_variation1.htm

count.) In other words, the smallest parts of us which are *not* seen are mostly identical—the features that are seen are somewhat different. What we are made of on the inside, is the very same stuff—few variations, and the superficial coverings are unique. Remember the old wise saying: "we all bleed red"? We'll that's an understatement—except for 0.01 percent we are identical.

The Apple and the Tree

We also see strong heredity of those superficial traits within a particular family: you are likely to resemble your close family members. We also see *intangible* personality (temperament) traits shared among family members.

We also see psychological traits shared within the entire human species, apparently controlled by shared hormones.

On the last point: observe the reaction of young teenage girls, from every single continent, to the teenaged male singing heartthrob. As a man, it has always amazed me that no matter the language, young girls will go into emotional hysteria over someone like Justin Beiber, or the current popular boy band. If you didn't know better, you would think you were watching footage from here in America. Similarly, I doubt there is a remote tribe in the world which doesn't join the rest of the world, in some kind of fanatical, competitive, male athletic competition. Madison Avenue's advertising industry understands the power of heredity, and relies on its laws to earn billions for their advertisers, through a single message targeted to tens of millions who share something in common—basic human nature, inherited from our ancestors. They bank on—with much success—the conviction that a very large percentage of us will respond in the *exact* same way: purchase the advertised product—for the reasons suggested in the advertisements.

> *"If the total paternal contribution to heredity is contained in a sperm cell, and the maternal in an egg, then this would have to not just involve the total anatomy and physiology of a human being, but also our numerous predispositions and gifts."* —Werner Gitt

Up to this point I have said a lot about the *involuntary* aspect of The Zone Phenomenon...essentially, **most** of what we experience is outside of our control. Professor Gitt in the quote above came to a similar conclusion after intensive study of human biology: the cell, mathematical probability, and DNA. He reasoned: we inherit *more* than just our physical traits, but also our inclinations and gifts.

This would explain the similarities between personalities, interests, and many other intangible traits of peoples all over the world. We are more alike than we are different, and heredity is responsible. **The source of the "seed" has a lot to do with the fruit produced.** As we have noted: this is more pronounced within close family members.

Heredity And Close Family

A remarkable example of very strong hereditary traits, perfectly suited for the task at hand—in this case war—was recorded around 1020 BC in the history of the Hebrew people. Of the 12 tribes of Israel, one tribe is described as follows:

> *"Among all this people there were seven hundred chosen men left-handed; every one could sling stones*

at an hair breadth, and not miss...and they were among the mighty men, helpers of the war.

And the children of Benjamin were numbered at that time out of the cities twenty and six thousand men that drew sword, beside the inhabitants of Gibeah, which were numbered seven hundred chosen men. Among all this people there were seven hundred chosen men lefthanded; every one could sling stones at an hair breadth, and not miss.

And of Benjamin; Eliada a mighty man of valour, and with him armed men with bow and shield two hundred thousand.

... and out of Benjamin, that bare shields and drew bows, two hundred and eighty thousand: all these were mighty men of valour. [11]

These men exhibited very strong hereditary traits, demonstrated as specialized talent, skill, or ability. There is no record of their general physical characteristics such as height or physique.

This historical account is a remarkable and unusual record—yet not unbelievable. These warriors were the offspring of a man named Benjamin, one of Jacob's (whose name was changed to Israel) descendents. Among his eleven siblings, an extremely large number (hundreds of thousands) of Benjamin's offspring possessed very strong physical traits: they were left-handed, ambidextrous warriors, expert fighters with bow and arrow, slinging stones, wielding sword and shield.

The most remarkable traits they all shared were: ***hair splitting accuracy*** with their weapons from a long distance,

---

[11] Judges 20:16; 1Ch 12:1; 1Ch 8:40; 2Ch 17:17; 2Ch 14:8

and the ability to use each hand with equal precision. Their inherited talents had to extend past shared physical characteristics into their senses of sight (including depth perception,) and touch, (the type of sensitivity in the fingertips required for precision tool handling.) The very strong genetically acquired abilities were passed on through generations including a very large number of siblings and cousins according to the history.[12]

That tribe demonstrates just how strong hereditary talents can be within a family. I am sure training plays a role in the **development** of a talent, but **perfecting** a skill through training is possible if your efforts are empowered by inherent talent.

∾

The incredible ability of the Benjamites is very unusual, yet I wouldn't say it is unbelievable. We have the contemporary story of the *Flying Wellenda* family of daredevil acrobats. Since 1904, the descendants of Karl Wellenda continue to amaze the world with their no-net high wire daredevil feats. Like the ancient Benjamites, the Wellenda's—no doubt—benefit from inheriting their patriarch's specialized genetic talents.

YOUR AREA OF TALENT?

I am amazed at how many people believe they have "no talent" to mention. This opinion is mostly due to what we define as talent. In 1983 Howard Earl Gardner a professor and developmental psychologist at Harvard University, published the

---

[12]King David, the giant slayer was a cousin to King Saul a Benjamite.

"Theory of Multiple Intelligences." Gardner, who has worked with "gifted" and "average" children, believes that everyone learns in different ways, based on their particular area of *"intelligence."*

This sounds like the laws of diversity, specialization, and gifts, doesn't it? I love it when we are careful to observe the law, especially when the signs are clearly posted.

Gardner identifies at least eight specific "intelligences", into which most people's gifts or talents would fit. He calls them intelligences because, to him, they each apply to essential areas which are just as **vital** to our lives, and the harmony of our world, as those the "IQ" test measures.

In my opinion, it is the height of arrogance for those with exceptional logic and reasoning abilities, to hold that ability as the standard by which everyone else's intelligence and **value** is to be measured. Those who lack a high level of mathematical, scientific, **memory**, or linguistic ability are considered less intelligent, less important, and therefore inferior. According to this theory, the great artist, dancer, parent, chef, and humanitarian, for example, have underachieved by failing to reach a higher level of intelligence supported by IQ scores.

It is an absolute fact that the world requires—better yet demands—skilled people in a broad range of critical areas, so as to function in a balanced and comprehensively productive way. If everyone chose science or law, the human race would have died off a very long time ago due to disease and malnutrition. Heaven knows we desperately need "diet" help these days, and are spending billions on treatments. Where would the celebrity diet guru of today rank on the standard IQ test?

I have to agree with Gardner's theory and can completely

understand how he was lead to this conclusion after working with both normal and gifted children—some with extraordinary and specialized abilities. My friend, I truly believe his assessment is the result of *absolute knowledge* acquired through simple observation of the facts of life.

WHAT ARE THE INTELLIGENCES

Gardner offers these areas of intelligence as a guide to identifying a person's basic area of talent. I believe this is a good starting reference for anyone looking to pinpoint their strengths or that of a child they want to point in the right direction.

LOGICAL-MATHEMATICAL: This intelligence involves logic, abstract thinking, reasoning, and numbers—not necessarily mathematical ability, but reasoning ability, recognizing abstract patterns, scientific thinking, investigative, and the ability to perform complex calculations. This is the 'intelligence" Jason Padgett (pg 47) instantly received a full measure of after being mugged and beaten. As I've suggested, I believe this "intelligence" is an essential ingredient in all *extraordinary* talent, it makes that gift very powerful—it's pure *oida (pg 62).*

SPATIAL: This area deals with spatial judgment, and the ability to visualize with the mind's eye. I would link this ability to a *strong sense of sight* (literally and or figuratively,) normally seen in artistic types; i.e. a strong sense of observation, and the relationship of one thing to another in space.

LINGUISTIC: This area has to do with words, spoken or written. People with high verbal, linguistic intelligence will have the preverbal "gift of gab", and a knack for all forms of communication. Be careful with this one, which is often received as an indication of superior intelligence and suitability for leadership: Great orator doesn't automatically equal great leader. Nonetheless, we all appreciate this talent on paper or spoken.

BODILY-KINESTHETIC: These people are generally good at physical activities such as sports or dance. They are very physically coordinated. Those Hebrew Benjamites, acrobats, dancers, athletes, craftsmen, etc., fit this category.

MUSICAL: This area has to do with sensitivity to sounds, rhythms, tones, and music. Mankind can absolutely not live without this talent.

INTERPERSONAL: They *communicate* effectively, *sympathize and empathize* easily with others, and may be either leaders or followers. Talents, not of the mouth, but of the soul and heart.

INTRA-PERSONAL: Thinkers, they are skillful at deciphering their own feelings and motivations. Likely interested in philosophy, health, psychology, etc. This refers to having a deeper *understanding of one's self.* No doubt some of us are driven to answer the deeper questions: who am I/we and why. An mere interest for all, but **obsession** for some.

NATURALISTIC: This area has to do with nurturing and relating information to one's natural surroundings. Attracted to areas such as agriculture, geology, astronomy, gardening, mining, etc. No doubt drawn to these areas through our worlds need for specialized knowledge in these areas.

I personally believe most of us have some combination of these abilities with at least one dominant. I suppose the possible combinations of intelligences are as infinite as the number of unique people there are on planet earth. Gardner's theory is an excellent and helpful guide but likely not complete: I believe it has been added to since its first appearance. Search him on the web for more detailed information.

The Logic of the Intelligences

Some critics of Gardner's theory object on the basis of "intelligence" being exclusively a mental function, including knowledge, reasoning, understanding, memory and learning. Functions which don't directly relate to processing and using information cannot therefore be correctly classified as "intelligent," they argue. I believe it is reasonable to classify *all* human beings as "a higher form of intelligence" compared to lower forms of intelligent life on earth. Our simplest functions are intelligent, even if they appear thoughtless and easy.

If the wonderful web-spinning spider exhibits a certain level of intelligence, certainly the skilled carpenter deserves to be recognized as highly intelligent. Whether or not the individual is able to skillfully articulate the intricacies of their area of talent, doesn't mean that intelligence, knowledge and understanding are not required in the performing of that task.

Ask the mathematician or scientist to put a new electrical outlet in his home, or handle the plumbing problems himself, and then tell me a high level of intelligence is not required to be proficient at those tasks. How about providing for your own entertainment—music, dance, comedy, sports...you get the point.

God forbid our hospitals lack staff with a high level of compassion and empathy. There are no doubt some people who have an innate understanding of human suffering, and are therefore drawn to healthcare for the purpose of relieving their neighbors misery from a heart that truly understands and cares. I will certainly acknowledge that kind of skill as highly intelligent, even if I lack the capacity to be moved by the misery of others in the same way. I can tell you one thing for sure: if we find ourselves at the mercy of a caretaker due to illness, we will all value what Gardner calls "interpersonal intelligence."

HARNESSED TALENT SPECIALIZATION

At the top level of any area of expertise, we can conclude that all of the performers are talented and have skills suited for that profession. A high degree of ability (natural or acquired through learning and training,) can get you to the top. Being at the top of your occupation or hobby of choice should be very rewarding because you have demonstrated a high level of achievement.

However, reaching and maintaining an extraordinary level of performance is reserved for those who have harnessed their *uniquely specialized* abilities. An even higher level of transcendence is reserved for *the few* who find and embrace their "diversity", and therefore set a new standard with their own *unique,* individual contribution. They have found, and/or have been found, by an endeavor for which their brain and body are particularly wired. By wiring I mean the synchronized collaboration between all body parts and systems to accomplish a task.

Your MAXIMUM Potential?

Because of our brain's tremendous ability to learn, and adapt to whatever task we put it to, we can do well at almost anything we determine to do—but that falls short of reaching full potential.

Take the game of chess, for example. Most of us have the capability to learn to play the game, and some of us will become very good chess players. However, our level of success will depend on our ability to **master all of the skills required** in the game.

According to Chess Basics by the U.S. Chess Federation and Peter Kurzdorfer,

> *"The skills required to play a strong chess game include the ability to visualize, the ability to memorize, the ability to recognize patterns, the ability to use analytic logic, the ability to plan ahead, the ability to make decisions, and the ability to accept the consequences of your actions."[13]*

Analytic logic involves three stages: learning from the past, diagnosing the present, and planning for the future. All are required to play good chess. (So genius level memory is not enough—interesting!)

It is my contention that the great players,[14] like Bobby Fischer, who was eight times US Champion, and many more titles around the world, and Gary Kasparov, (at the age of 22 the youngest chess champion in history, at that time,) possessed all of the skills required to play the game of chess. They possessed these skills in abundance, and to a high degree of proficiency, which allowed them to beat other skilled players, who may have been lacking one or more of the key skills needed to dominate.

Working in an area you are innately gifted for, or to which

---

[13] netplaces.com/chess-basics/

[14] http://coxschess.tripod.com/greatest.html

your innate talents are suited, is *a key* for access into The Zone of extraordinary human performance. It is what separates the 'great-ones" from the rest.

FIND YOUR TALENT EARLY

This specialized wiring usually manifests itself at an early age, when the brain is feverishly forging those unique connections that will make us who we are, and laying the foundation for who we can become as an adult...our *potential* as we mature. It all starts early.

Very early in childhood development some children are more inclined toward creative and imaginative pursuits, while others gravitate toward analytical interest: "Mommy why this, Mommy why that?" These children instinctively want to know how things fit together, and what they mean in relation to other things.

Some children have a strong social connection, and are able to sympathize and empathize with the feelings and suffering of others. They may even express a strong sense of family, friendship and community, while others are loners. Other children have a strong desire for adventure that manifests in exploration, in and out of the textbooks. Some children have a love for sports that began very early in their development. Others are recognized and accepted by their peers as natural leaders. Some show an interest and ability in art or music.

As parents, teachers, and coaches, we make a mistake if we ignore the natural tendencies, interests, and talents of the children we influence, and attempt to force them toward careers and occupations for which they are not suited, have little interested, and therefore, are less likely to excel at. Since this book is about outstanding performance, I am not talking about doing well. Instead, I'm talking about **maximum potential** as a result of specialization.

This *early in life* timetable is confirmed by the fact that the human brain has reached approximately 93% of its full development by the time we reach first grade, somewhere around the age of six.[15] This means most of those brain networks are in place. All that is left are the networks forged by experience or maturity.

> "The child's brain begins developing within a couple of weeks of conception. Neurologists estimate that between 50,000 and 100,000 new brain cells are generated each second between the fifth and twentieth weeks of birth. (No wonder that new-born sleeps so much.) The brain will grow to about 80 percent of the adult size by the age of 3 and 90 percent by the age of 5."[16]

Therefore, depending on the child's unique genetic wiring, he or she most certainly will begin to demonstrate some area of special ability, focus, or interest at an early age. Sometimes the neural pathways may be strong enough that the child will demonstrate a prodigious (genius) level of understanding and capability in a particular area. After all, his brain is 93% developed. The only difference between his brain and his mother or father's brain is 7% additional growth, learning, and life experience, which ingrain knowledge, preferences, and patterns.

If this is in fact true, it is no wonder child prodigies usually manifest their extraordinary abilities around the age of five

---

[15] Dr. Jay N. Geidd, Imaging The Developing Brain, UCTV
[16] www.firststeps.us/parents_braindevelopment.shtml

or sooner. The only logical explanation for this level of ability at such an early age is specialization, gift, or innate talent.

Professional golfer J. B. Holmes, in an interview on The Golf Channel's *Playing Lessons from the Pros,* said he has the same swing now that he had when he was five years old. It seems that after first picking up a golf club at the age of 14 months, and beginning to swing, his brain perfected the pathways for his particularly unusual method of swinging; so that by the time his brain was 90% developed around the age of five, it had forged the networks that would serve him into physical maturity and his professional golf career. For him, a foundation for athletic performance, laid during his first 60 months of life was good enough to build upon (specialization), eventually taking him to the top of professional golf.

The same is true for young prodigies in other disciplines—a few of which we looked at in early chapters. The neural networks for their talent are ***extremely*** powerful at a very early age. (Just today on a national talk show there was a 13 year old music prodigy who first began to recognize words at 6 months old.)

"Little Stevie Wonder" demonstrated remarkable musical maturity in his first hit record *"Fingertips".*[17] I will venture to say: at the age of 11 he was as musically brilliant as he is today. I am not sure that in his entire illustrious career he has outdone the instinctive brilliance of that first hit record. It was a masterful combination of compositional genius, musical performance, combined with an unusual ability to engage his audience.

Another example of early demonstration of music talent

---

[17]Read some interesting details: http://en.wikipedia.org/wiki/Fingertips

is Keith Jarrett, the successful Jazz musician who, **before the age of three**, demonstrated what is referred to as absolute pitch (AP or perfect pitch). AP is the ability to name or reproduce a tone without reference to an external standard.[18] In other words, he was either born with the ability or rapidly (somewhere between birth and his first 36 months on earth) acquired the ability to perfectly repeat tones and notes. He also started piano lessons before his third birthday.

This is incredible to me, an average person, who enjoys music of all types, but I have little ability to recognize broad—not to mention—subtle differences between tones and sounds.

The most reasonable way to explain these examples, is that the wiring in these children's brains (Keith Jarrett's for example, 80% developed at age three,) are more fully developed (compared to other children and most adults) in the particular areas related to sound or music, and they just happened to discover or demonstrate their particular innate area of specialized talent at a very, very, early age—while many of us miss it altogether or discover it much later.

Think of what would have happened if their parents insisted on them becoming lawyers or baseball players? These guys would have no doubt put their brain to it and become successful, but would have missed their true potential.

Physical Talents Blossom Later

Now, if J. B. Holmes's arms were 90% of their adult size at the age of five, we would expect a "Baby Huey" or "Bam Bam" type of strength from the toddler, but unfortunately physical development is much slower.

---

[18] http://en.wikipedia.org/wiki/Keith_Jarrett

Since most prodigies lie in non-athletic areas, it's like being super strong, except not in the body, but in the brain. J. B. Holmes, although a talented child golfer, couldn't compete with adults yet; but Matt Savage (chp 4) the music prodigy could, because strong muscles are not necessary to play piano.

The Logic of Sticking With It?

Allow me to digress for the purpose of extracting some meaning. In light of J. B. Holmes' staying with a single swing method from childhood, more light is shed on Tiger Woods' "rewired" golf swing.

Remember, most *experts* said the third and most recent overhaul would prove disastrous to Tiger's golf career. They were theoretically right, but we know theory and practice don't always agree. Logic says: through consistent and repeated use, a skill will improve. It was so for J. B. and Tiger during their rise to the professional level. But, you change the pattern, re-direct the wiring, alter the route to the destination, and it is *unlikely* you will be able to reach your destination with the same proficiency as before.

The Law of the Learning Curve (#5)

The biggest reason many critics discredited Sean Foley's methods was—in my opinion—ignorance of how learning takes place. Tiger, the once dominant golfer, was having a very difficult time incorporating the new methods, which was *perceived* by many observers as failure.

The first reason Tiger was experiencing difficulty (we've discussed in several places previously), is the powerful principle of pruning. After selecting the most proficient, efficient pathway to accomplishing a task, the brain goes through a pruning process, reducing the number of connections along a pathway by pruning unneeded connections. This process creates unwillingness in the brain to accept change, because hopefully, through trial and error, by process of elimination, and approving the correct methods: **there is no need to change what has been established.** You may be familiar with the wise proverb, which speaks to the power of ingrained habits:

"A leopard can't change his spots..."

Therefore, if it becomes necessary to **rebuild** pathways to performing a task once perfected (due to age, injury, discovery of more efficient methods, etc.,) expect it to be a difficult task. **Expect therapy: mental, physical, and likely, emotional.**

We can add to the law of *The Learning Curve*: THE LAW OF PERSEVERANCE.

Tiger has disproved popular theory, and is number one in the world again, and it appears he will remain in that vicinity for a while, as neural networks are pruned, and new ones reinforced.

I like this scenario, because it proves that although the rule is: "you can't teach an old dog new tricks," there is an exception—"*Where there's a will, there's a pathway.*" Albeit, that "will" must be accompanied by specialized talent, founded on knowledge of what is possible with the resources we possess. Application? Theoretical rules, and the history of other individual's performance cannot trump innate talent, guided by knowledge?

TALENTS HAVE SEVERAL APPLICATIONS

Simply because my family and I have strong artistic ability, doesn't mean, if I want to be "all that I can be" I am confined to a career as an artist. Although, it is a fact that a career in art could very well produce an opportunity for me to reach a level of performance above the average artist because of my inherited gift. But, because my set of talents will be different from my family members, it is likely I will have other dominant or complimentary talents received from somewhere in my ancestry—remember how recombination of genes guarantees each child is unique.

For example, my artistic ability allows me to not only see the relationship between the visual shapes of objects in the world, but in a very similar way I see the relationship between concepts and ideas. Similar to the way my mind appreciates the harmony between visual objects (I have a natural aversion to random abstract art,) I very often recognize disharmony between intellectual ideas and concepts in which I am interested. I am a strong visual learner, so I instinctively convert everything I'm learning into shapes, and connecting lines. It is very much like assembling puzzle pieces together...looking for shapes that fit together, and recognizing those which don't; although, we are talking about ideas instead of objects. (I know a musician would distinguish sounds in the same way. And a talented mathematician would likely calculate things numerically.) This is no-doubt inherited ability.

Therefore, I may do well, and reach a high level of performance in an occupation other than art, where an ability to harmonize intellectual ideas and concepts is a premium, such as non-fiction writing.☺ The point is that a person's talents

and abilities can flourish in areas that—to other observers—
are not *obviously* related. This is also a result of the law of
diversity.

Intelligences and Senses

I noticed that some of Gardner's intelligences may be explained by one of the five senses being dominant in an individual, thereby creating a strong intelligence in specific areas
of life and vocation. This makes sense, and may be the result
of genes or well developed areas of the brain which relate to
that particular sense. (It appears a fact to me that, the greater
number of senses involved in a talent the greater the performance will be.)

It is unlikely that every human being has the same level
of development, and degree of sensitivity to the five senses.
Some are bound to have better vision, leading not just to
sharper and precise eyesight, but more sensitivity to colors,
shapes, light, etc. It is a fact that a significant portions of the
population are color blind, and have weaker vision. Many of
us are physically uncoordinated, while others can perform
acrobatics with ease. Some hear notes, others are tone deaf.
Great chefs have powerful senses of smell and taste.

If there is in fact a connection between Gardner's theory
and our five senses (six if we add the "heart" to cover interpersonal intelligence), it would be easier to pinpoint a person's
dominant intelligence or area of talent.

One Dominant Trait, Many Manifestations

On the idea of talent manifesting in a seemingly unrelated
area, I noticed this fact as I studied savants with different ex-

traordinary gifts, which on the surface seemed unrelated— art, math, dates and calendars, music, and memory. **The experts note that all savants have an incredible memory in common.** (I've noticed the same with child prodigies and geniuses.) This is a characteristic of the phenomenon, and is an essential ingredient in producing their incredible gifts. Memory can be a talent? I digress.

It appears to me that they also all share a mastery and understanding of basic mathematical concepts. Possibly the same area of the brain is affected, but the *manifestation* is different based on other complimentary factors (talents), or how this pivotal area relates to other areas of the brain:

The Power of Observation

Each of the gifts savants exhibit is intricately tied to the ability to observe and calculate relationships between things. Artistic ability calculates the geometrical and spatial relationship between objects. Combine this ability with a flawless memory, and a brain wired to output this perception down the spinal cord and through the hands, and you have an artistic savant. **Math+Visual Observation+Memory+Touch=Artistic Savant**

The Power of Hearing

The music savant, instead of an extraordinary power of sight, has a transcendent power of hearing—in a flawless, harmonious, and rhythmic way (i.e. sounds and notes, and their mathematical relationship to each other.) You combine this ability with a flawless memory, and a brain wired to output this perception down the spinal cord, and out through the

hands, and you have a music savant, with the ability to reproduce Mozart on piano after a single hearing, with no training.
Math+Hearing+Memory+Touch=Music Savant

The math savant appears to have all of his brain power
concentrated on mathematics, without the added tie-in to
the senses of sight, taste, touch or sound (although, some see
numbers as colors and shapes indicating some relationship
with sight.) They exhibit the raw brain power of effortless nu-
merical knowledge without calculation—they just know the
answer to the equation without thinking, or with little effort.

**This comparison illustrates that one dominate trait—in
this case mathematical ability, can express itself in a number of different ways when tied in with one of the five senses.**

The same is most likely true of *your* inherent talent or ability. It may be expressed differently from your family members
based on which of your senses are the strongest.

My brother uses his share of the family's artistic genes to
play guitar—he's got an ear for music. Like me, he has enjoyed
his talent since we were kids.

I have a nephew who exhibited an uncanny love for sports
at a very early age. Somewhere around the age of eight he
would argue basketball or football like he was a seasoned
adult. My sister married a man under six feet tall, so with my
family inheriting similar stature my nephew has slim chance
of making it as a professional basketball player. But, it is very
possible that his love for sports may translate into some other
area of the sports world? His understanding of the dynamics
of the games is well suited for a career as a coach or com-

mentator, for example; possibly even some other occupation requiring strategic analytic ability.

TALENT • UNDERSTANDING • CHECKMATE!

I believe Tiger's innate talent involves more than the physical ability to swing a golf club along a repeated path. It must—like chess—involve an understanding of many systems connected to the game of golf. The physical, mental, and related systems, he sees and understands to a greater degree than most athletes and experts in his sport.

His broad understanding of golf, reminds me of the natural ability and insight of chess greats like Magnus Carlsen, the youngest Chess Grand Champion, who sees **12 or 20 moves ahead**. Magnus is not only able to see his next 15 moves, but his opponents' options and possible responses—options and possible responses for each of the next 15 moves. Additionally, the scope of his vision (all that his mind sees) at a given moment, includes:

- His training
- Past experience
- Knowledge of his opponents' tendencies
- Historical information from great matches
- Information in front of him
- Raw intuition
- And things that are possible

Not to mention what he knows of his opponent. This kind of extraordinary perception, memory, and calculating power, illustrate my original theory regarding one common aspect of TZP—"rapid processing of new and stored information." What if Magnus calculates chess options at the blazing speed at which Daniel Tamment or Rüdiger Gamm calculate complex math problems?

Although not as spontaneous—yet very much like Magnus—Tiger draws upon his very broad, deep knowledge, and understanding of the game of golf, to outperform his competitors, and increase his winning percentage.

How so?

Magnus is known to **"sacrifice a queen"** (chess's most powerful piece) in battle, in order to eventually win the war many moves later. Innate talent that synchronizes all of the brain's resources, producing remarkable performance in a given area, allows the individual to see with the mind, not only the possibilities, but the limitations in the options.

During one match, Magnus sacrificed his Queen; His opponent and spectators thought it was a misstep against a capable opponent. But it was calculated wisdom, based on broader, further vision, and deeper knowledge, which became shockingly apparent several moves later...Checkmate!

Likewise, when Tiger decided to "sacrifice his queen," i.e., to scrap his old swing system, and file for bankruptcy reorganization, his opponents, golf experts, and many fans thought it was a fatal misstep for sure. However, it has proven to be checkmate.

Exceptional talent encompasses the being wherein it resides: the vision, the mind, including the understanding, creating the ability to see possibilities hid from the sight of others. This is also the power of specialization in action.

GENERAL OBSERVATION ON THE LAW OF HEREDITY

Mastering More Than One Ability

When we factor in "specialization," the difficulty of **mastering** more than one ability becomes obvious. As I mention elsewhere (pg. 150), the more related the abilities, the greater the possibility of mastering them both. Conversely, the less related the activities, the less likely it is to master them both.

By the way, "straight A's" in school is no indication of exceptional ability across the board, it is likely evidence of a good memory, that's all.

Shaping Talent

There is no doubt everyone is able to shape or influence their inherent talents through personal experience, or as scientists classify them "environmental factors." I'm five feet eight, one hundred seventy five pounds, but if I over eat (environmental factor), no matter what my family's genetics dictate, I can pack on another 100 pounds. I can also pack on another 50 pounds of muscle if I train with weights. I can learn to distinguish musical notes and sing—perhaps:-) I can take drugs and alter the way my brain works by disrupting its delicate chemical balance and cripple my artistic ability. I can starve my brain of water and nutrients through a poor diet. All of these things will change the way my inherited abilities are manifested, or whether they manifest at all. You get the point.

Talent Compels

I believe we are *compelled* in the genetic fiber of our being, when we discover and are drawn toward activities and endeavors for which we find ourselves exceptionally suited. Did you know that Dwayne Johnson's (aka The Rock's) father and grandfather were also professional wrestlers? One may love the sport, and desire to get in the ring, but suitable genes could be the difference between thriving or merely surviving.

One professor of psychology[19], a leading authority on genetics tells a story of a "eminent amateur ornithologist" who discovered that he was adopted around the age of 11. He found that he had inherited his lifelong *interests* as well as *talents* from his biological parents, and had very little, in the way of abilities and interests, in common with his adoptive parents. The power of innate genetic abilities had an overwhelming influence over him compared to his adoptive family upbringing and their shared interests. **Heredity in this case, was much more powerful than environment or experience.**

This truth is played out all the time when family members separated at an early age are reunited many years later. In 2012 Olympic medal-winning gymnast Dominique Moceanu found out for the first time she had a younger sister (Jennifer) who was also an accomplished gymnast—as well as one of her biggest fans. Obviously, there was a strong tendency toward athletic artistry in their genes compelling them toward kinesthetic artistry in gymnastics—quite a remarkable story.

January 9, 2013 the Jeter sisters, separated as infants, met for the first time after 17 years, at a local track meet. The sisters not only looked alike but share double jointed thumbs, a

---

[19] *The Genetics of Genius*, David T. Lykken

fondness for track, and they talk alike: so much so that friends can't tell them apart on the phone.[20] These traits were obviously not learned but **ingrained** on their inherited genes.

Concentration, Focus, Obsession

Talent can be so powerful a force that it pushes or draws the child into that area of performance. The documentary "Perfect Pitch" shares the testimony of a couple of musically talented individuals who are obsessed with identifying every sound and noise they hear. *In my opinion this is an extremely important observation on the manifestation of talent. When obsession is present it is a key indicator of innate talent. However, the possible areas of talent have to be broad enough to recognize subtle signs from such talents such as* Gardner's *'intra and inter-personal" intelligences.*

Bobby Fischer, arguably the greatest American chess player in history, when asked what it takes to be a great chess player, said:

> *"It seems to me, in chess, you have to have the talent but the guys who reach the top are the ones who keep at it, have the character, they don't get distracted by other things in life until they got the title...or whatever they wanted out of chess"...Q: "can you have any other life and be a great chess player?" Fischer: "Not at the moment, no, first things first right, get the title."*

At the time Mr. Fischer made that statement, he had not yet reached number one in the world; he was the best American chess player, looking higher up the mountain, calculating

---

http://www.usatoday.com/story/news/nation/2013/05/13/sisters-reunited-track-meet/2155751/

how much he had already spent, and how much more it would cost to reach the top.

Concentration

Some time ago while attempting to teach a young relative how to draw, I observed what I perceived to be a lack of concentration on his part. (I've added concentration to my keys to The Zone. It has an obvious connection to talent and gifts also.) You may not realize how much concentration or focus is required to accomplish a task that comes easy for you, until you try to teach someone else how to do it.

When I would instruct my potential artist to draw the flower vase sitting on the table, I noticed concentration was difficult for him. First of all, I know that we are both seeing the same thing with our eyes, so any difference in what we draw is not a result of seeing two different things. (I am assuming we both have fairly good eyesight.)

Invariably, my non-artistic students would draw a distorted object. So my next step was to make sure they have the *ability* to draw simple but different lines and shapes. So, I would instruct them to draw (after my example), a straight horizontal line, a straight vertical line, a bottom left to upper right diagonal line, a half circle, a full circle, a square, a rectangle, and a triangle. With little to no trouble, they were all able to accomplish this task, and differentiate the lines and shapes.

The problem arose, I noticed, when they have to put all of these shapes together to draw an object. The gifted artist sees the interactions and relationships between lines and shapes, which form visual objects. Guess what? The non-artist sees these shapes and lines also, but lacks the ability to draw what he sees. Instead of the half circle shape within the vase, they may draw a half oval shape. Instead of the irregular shape of an apple, they will draw a circle.

The non-artist *feels it tedious* to follow every different change of line direction and shape, and their relationship to each other—it is beyond their ability *or desire* to focus on those details. **They lack the patience, concentration, and interest for that task. Or, I believe, their brains are not wired for it. Their area of specialization or talent lies elsewhere.**

~

My wife, a gifted and talented singer, was one of my art students. Her attempts to teach me to hear the difference between music notes while attempting to sing were just as futile. I can hear the beautiful music and melody, but am unable to detect and repeat different notes and tones. My hearing and vocal systems are not as strong as my seeing and touch systems. **The failure is not in the *hearing*, it is in the *processing* of what I hear.** It is as though my brain stops somewhere after the hearing, while my wife's brain starts with the sound, and sends it to her vocal center, as well as other areas, for a much fuller understanding of what the sound *means,* and how it can and should be used.

Because music is difficult for me, I am unwilling to apply the focus, concentration, and effort it would take to learn and to distinguish tones. Truthfully, I may never be able to accomplish that task, to the level that people would enjoy my singing. A person with music talent would cringe at my efforts.

My brain is wired visually and artistically (drawing), and my wife's brain is wired for hearing and vocalizing. Did you notice we both have at least two senses working powerfully together? Therefore, our respective areas of talent are easy for us, and require very little effort. It is as though when she hears music, her ears automatically tune-in and understand the language, and her vocal cords are ready and able to respond as well. While for me, when I see things, I automatically see the relationship between the objects, shapes and lines. Another interesting observation is: what harmony is to music—pleasing and harmonious—pleasant shapes are to my artistic eye.

Talent and the 10,000 Hour Theory

Why did Larry Bird spend so much time practicing after he became a great basketball player? Didn't he need that practice and concentration to maintain his exceptional performance? Let's move on to answer these questions.

This controversial theory states that the great performers got that way, not because of any inherent genetic advantage, but because they have dedicated at least 10,000 hours of intense practice. Performance will succeed in accordance with the number of hours you practice: 8,000 hours will produce good, not great, results, 5000 will produce average, etc., the theory goes.

> *"The distinctive characteristics of exceptional performers are the result of adaptations to extended and intense practice activities that selectively activate dormant genes that are contained within all healthy individuals' DNA." —Ericsson et al., NYAS, 1172: 199-217, 2009*

Dr. K. Anders Ericsson, Department of Psychology, Florida State University believes "dormant" genes are not activated below the 10,000 hours of training threshold. Those dormant genes evidently trigger greatness or exceptional performance.

Everyone has the same abilities, but only the very hard trainers tap into those abilities, Ericsson believes. Malcolm Gladwell made the theory more popular recently, through his best-selling book *Outliers*.

There are a number of criticisms of this theory online from scientists, athletes, and musicians, so I won't rehash all of them here. The observations and facts I've already shared regarding diversity and specialization powerfully contradict the idea that everyone has the same exact genetic wiring and "potential."

The 10,000 hour theory attempts to remove a fear of "the haves and have nots", by teaching: if you work hard you can have the same success as the "great ones." We've learned that even identical twins with apparently **identical DNA,** have different abilities; so even in this extreme case, no two people produce the same performance.

You can take all of the time you want to train and practice…10,000-20,000 hours, and you will never be the natural entertainer that Michael Jackson was. He was the epitome of raw music entertainment talent. Under the same training, life experiences, guidance, resources, and opportunities, his own brothers never came close to equaling the gifts he exhibited.

The Jackson family (other talented families could be sited e.g. Osmond's, Bee Gees, etc.) are a testament to the fact that heredity and hard work can make you successful. Each human being (the epitome of intelligent life on earth) is capable of doing nearly anything we put our minds to, and be good at it. But this does not rise to the level of transcendence we see in The Zone Phenomena of extraordinary performance, or in the exploits of those at the top of their profession or craft.

226 | UNCONSCIOUS: Secrets of The Zone...

So, you want to spend ten thousand hours of practice and training, because you want to be the next Mozart? Without prodigious innate talent, your efforts, while they will bear some fruit, will fall far short of your aspirations, and therefore be futile.

Hard Work and Drive

Why did Larry Bird, the basketball great, practice so hard?

The supporters of the 10,000 hour theory of high performance will point to a number of top performers as proof of the theory, and as inspiration for those who aspire to follow in their footsteps. The truth is: a number of factors come together to drive the ambition of top performers at a very early age, resulting in thousands of hours of practice. These factors include:

- A strong perception of the area of interest: an ability to understand the dynamics of its operations, various aspects and components. An instinctive understanding of the area of interest.

- Early success in performing the fundamental tasks related to the interest—skillful performance. This is a "taste of success" which fuels the insatiable thirst for more success.

- A desire to reach the level of perfection the talented individual perceives as within reach, based on their level of talent and skill. When you are Larry Bird and a Magic Johnson comes along, the level of perfection has suddenly nudged upward. What do you do with your considerable talent? You nudge it upward to meet the demand, through practice, training, and learning. When extraordinary becomes less extraordinary, the extraordinary raise the bar even higher—if they can.

- The expectation of even more improvement from training, practice, and experience. You don't know what's possible until you test the limits. So, the great-ones forge ahead.

This is what drives thousands of hours of hard work. When you hear interviews with exceptional people who began as children, they unanimously say they enjoyed training and practice, often dragging their parents to practice. This is "specialization" at work, as they are drawn to function in an area where their specialized gifts can be utilized to maximum potential.

On the other hand, when a child is pushed by parents into a particular area in which they are not interested, the result—sometimes good—will most likely fall short of exceptional. This explains why many child prodigies drop out of their area of talent as adults, and opt for different occupations. Had the prodigy been allowed to choose his own course, he may have chosen another avenue to utilize the same talent, or taken a slower pace in the same field.

> *...every hands a potential winner, and every hands a potential loser—the secret to thriving is knowing what to throw away, and knowing what to keep...*
> —*Modified lyrics, The Gambler,* **Kenny Rogers**

Unrealistic Expectations: The Crisis

Why not work on it until I break through if I can do well at anything I put my mind to? Because a dangerous by-product of unrealistic expectations, is psychological and emotional problems resulting from *disappointment, failure, and unsatisfied expectations.*

Unfortunately, we don't often hear about the emotional and psychological effects of ambition that ended in failure, because the successes are publicized, celebrated…and they sell news. Only the families and close friends get to witness the disappointment of the misguided dreamer.

You know the way I see the well-known **"mid life crises"** theory/phenomena? It's a man finding out in his forties he's been pursuing the wrong thing. He has found a gaping hole in his development, which he now is compelled to stop and fill-up or fill-in. He has reached a point of despair, having forged a course for which is finds himself unsuited. Or, he recognizes another path for which he thinks himself better suited.

It is best to establish your expectations and plans, based on your ability to meet the necessary requirements for the goal. Do I have what it takes to be as good as Mozart? Is this a rational expectation? Are my talents and equipment comparable to my anticipated competition in that area?

Heredity, Specialization and Diversity Summarized

Heredity from our ancestors or parents is responsible for all human performance, and we are involuntary recipients of this gift. The reality of this powerful law should also serve to discourage jealousy as well as pride, because we understand that the apple can't be greater than the seed which produced it. This is not the: which came first the apple or the seed debate; But, we know that each person is the product of their ancestors seed—no matter the greatness of their talent it was *derived* from their ancestors. In this light, the offspring cannot be greater than the parents, even if their talent appears to say otherwise. The parent cannot pass on what they do not possess. The only exception would be a miracle, an inexplicable gift.

Specialization gives the individual the broad capacity to understand an area of talent with their eyes, hands, heart, brain, and mind. Diversity gives him/her the desire and courage to bring their own individual, unique contribution to the table, (each person is in fact unique). Together they can produce a type of transcendence witnessed at its highest potential in The Zone.

Diversity and Specialization are necessary for the world to function on all levels—**embrace them, they are the law.**

CHAPTER ELEVEN

Inexplicable Talent: Gifts

"...Render to Caesar the things that are Caesar's, and to God the things that are God's...."
—Jesus

N ow that we've looked (mostly) at the genetic distribution of abilities, let's fix our focus on those incidences of re- markable ability which don't appear to come from Mom, Dad, or any ancestor. This kind of ability may well be de- scribed as an unearned, fortuitous gift. It is a gift because it is considered to be a special, valuable, endowment from a *super-* natural source. Don't be afraid of the phrase "super-natural", it simply means, without a identifiable *natural* cause—in this case, no family history of the talent.

The word talent sometimes means the same thing as gift, but has come to describe the ability itself, without any refer- ence to how it was acquired.

Involuntary Privilege: Beneficium

Speaking of inexplicable talent and gift, we must keep in mind *Law #1* of The Zone: *Beneficium.*

I am reminded of the enigma known as Bo Jackson, who threatened to nullify the laws of specialization & diversity by producing Hall of Fame performance in both Major League Baseball and the NFL. His exploits are the thing of comic book super hero legend—too many to recount here, plus, you will want to see them for yourself. To my knowledge none of his numerous siblings (or any of his peers for that matter) shared his extreme athletic ability. Another interesting note: Bo didn't practice, he hated it—pure innate talent![1]

Quite often an individual will take credit, in the form of pride and arrogance, for their exceptional ability or talent, attributing it to training, determination, etc. But, I am convinced even those instances are essentially "beneficium: involuntary privilege™, because we control very little that happens in this life. By the way, Bo attributed his extraordinary talents to God.

We have seen the extraordinary savants who, to a man, attribute their abilities to something other than themselves, or an act of their own will. We have observed that the athlete and artisan, temporarily experiencing TZP, will not and cannot attribute the experience to self-will either. Therefore, they all imply their special endowment is a gift.

"Was Mozart ever asked how he does this? I would be very impressed if he had a good answer to that. Because I think what he would say is

---

[1] See video on Bo Jackson's feats: http://goo.gl/ClqnQM

that it just comes natural to me. It's what I do"
—"The Mozart of Chess" Magnus Carlsen

Specialization a Gift from the Manufacturer

This leads us to consider such a thing as **God-given talent**. Sometimes the occasion and circumstances of super human performance defy any logical or scientific explanation, *forcing us* into the "super natural" realm for answers.

There is an interesting historical account that would support this conclusion: It is the record of the building of the ancient Hebrew people's elaborate religious tabernacle. It would require specialized knowledge and skills to construct *the tabernacle*, all of its furnishings, and the garments of those men who would carry out the special religious service. The details were exact, and had to be followed precisely. At that time the Hebrew people were fresh out of slavery in Egypt (around 1446 BC):

"And Jehovah spoke to Moses, saying: Behold, I have called by name Bezaleel, the son of Uri, the son of Hur, to the tribe of Judah. And I have filled him with the spirit of God in wisdom, and in intelligence, and in knowledge, and in all workmanship, to devise designs, to work in gold and in silver and in bronze, and in cutting of stones for finishings, and in carving of wood, to work in all workmanship. And behold! I have given with him Aholiab the son of Ahisamach of the tribe of Dan; and in the heart of every wise-hearted one I have given wisdom; and they shall make all which I have commanded you: the tabernacle of the congregation, and the ark of the testimony, and the mercyseat which is going up over it, and all the vessels of the tabernacle, and the table and its vessels, and the pure lampstand and all its vessels, and the altar of incense;

*and the altar of burnt offering and all its vessels,
and the laver and its base; and the woven garments,
and the holy garments for Aaron the priest, and the
garments of his sons, to minister as priests; and the
oil of anointing, and the incense of perfumes for the
sanctuary; according to all which I have commanded
you, they shall do."[2]*

For those of us looking for an explanation to the puzzle of talent, gifts, diversity and specialization, and are inclined to look for answers (for which current authorities have none,) from above, we may find answers in the above quote.

If Bezaleel and Aholiab were alive today and all of a sudden demonstrated that kind of ability, they would be called at least geniuses, or most likely acquired prodigious savants. Although in this case, they received a gift—the source of which was directly from God. History records the details of the elaborate Tabernacle, furnishings, and religious services, which resulted from Bezaleel's and Aholiab's gifts; it was their place of worship for hundreds of years.

Another well known example of God-given ability is the record of King Solomon and his legendary wisdom. Many of his ideas and thoughts are preserved in writing today in proverbs, songs, and philosophical writings, as well as third party accounts. His gifts would include at least five of the eight areas of "intelligence" identified by Professor Howard Earl Gardner: Logical, Spatial, Linguistic, Intrapersonal, and Musical.

*And God gave Solomon exceeding great wisdom and
understanding, and largeness of heart, even as the
sand that is on the seashore. And Solomon's wisdom
was greater than the wisdom of all the sons of the
east, and all the wisdom of Egypt. For he was wiser*

---

[2] Exodus 31:1-11

than all men; ... And his fame was in all nations all around. And he spoke three thousand proverbs, and his songs were a thousand and five. And he spoke of trees, from the cedar tree in Lebanon even to the hyssop that springs out of the wall. He spoke also of beasts and of birds, and of creeping things, and of fish. And there came from all the people, to hear the wisdom of Solomon, from all the kings of the earth, who had heard of his wisdom.[3]

How Can One Know What He Hasn't Learned

Before you dismiss the above quotes as fantasy and religious fiction, consider that we have already heard from great composers and musicians, who attributed their talent to divine inspiration (*Musical Inspiration* pg. 22ff). So, it is not incredible that exceptional talent or skill be attributed to a source outside of that person, specifically their creator.

Dr. Darold A. Treffert, in his excellent book *Islands of Genius*, a detailed discussion on savants, raised this question:[4] How can savants instantly know things, on a genius level, which they have never been taught or studied? He was referring to knowledge of the complex rules of music, art, and mathematics. He questioned if these skills are somehow "innate," because of their *sudden* appearance in those like "acquired/sudden" savants, (who, as a result of some event become genius—like Jason Pagett, pg. 47).

One reasonable explanation for that which is inexplicable—by any reasonable natural cause—is a super natural (spiritual) cause. Not so farfetched for us, whose very exis-

---

[3] 1Kings 4
[4] Introduction pg. 12

tence can be reasonably described as phenomenal, compared to other manufactured things on planet earth.

Whether or not you are inclined to attribute the demonstration of super-natural talent or ability to God, it is nevertheless a fact that some people exhibit abilities which defy our explanation and understanding (see *Permanent Residents*). Add the laws of diversity and specialization, and the suggestion of intentional purpose forces us to consider God as the source, opposed to something unintelligent and purposeless.

The Gift to Teach

Commenting on how music ability relates to heredity: *The Journal of Heredity Vol.7* states:

> *"I think it is a matter of heredity, but that almost everyone possesses the heredity. Twenty years of teaching give me reason to believe that, although great genius will doubtless continue to be sporadic and unaccountable, real musical ability is much more common than has been supposed."*

This conclusion, based on many years experience teaching young people how to play music, is no surprise if we accept the facts discussed in this book. Mainly, the super ability of our brains to *learn and do* well at whatever we apply it to. But we are seeking to understand that "sporadic" *higher level*, which the journal calls "great genius," and we are associating with "The Zone Phenomenon."

Perhaps the writer's confidence in his *ability to teach*, has as much to do with his conviction that music ability is innate within everyone, and his success in teaching reinforced this belief.

I would argue that the ability to teach is itself *a gift* which some have a greater portion of:

> And He has put in his heart that he may **teach**, he and Aholiab the son of Ahisamach, of the tribe of Dan. He has filled them with wisdom of heart to work all kinds of work; of the smith, and of the skillful worker, and of the embroiderer, in blue, and in purple, in scarlet, and in bleached linen, and of the weaver, of those who do any work, and of those who work out artful work.[5]

The above quote is a continuation of the historical narrative on God's gifts to Bezaleel we previously discussed. Here, the ability to teach was *added* to the gift of skillful craftsmanship; a "practice what you teach" or vise versa scenario.

The ability to teach is interesting, in that it requires a very high level of knowledge of the subject, an understanding of the process of human learning, and effective methods of imparting knowledge and skill to students. The teacher must be able to encourage and initiate the forging of new pathways in the brain, for the achievement of whatever skill or knowledge that is to be learned. A perfect example of a true gift to teach is found in exceptional parents. This occupation is common but the exceptionally gifted are rare. Yet, all of the qualities of a good teacher can be found in them.

The above quote from scripture describes the gift as "filled...with wisdom of heart...," which suggests a deeper, beyond the head, knowledge. We often *overlook* these essential skills which accompany exceptional teachers, and mistakenly elevate the high achiever to the position of teacher simply because he/she has been, or is, successful in some area. Like the top salesman promoted to sales manager, in hopes he

---

[5] Exodus 35;30 ff

will be able to transfer his success to others. These days we see this mistake more often demonstrated when a successful athlete, entertainer or business person is promptly elevated to "life coach", and encouraged to teach the world the secrets of success. In our example of parenting, I'm sure we all know successful people who are unsuccessful parents, and therefore poor teachers at home. These considerations should also serve as a guide for anyone looking for a mentor to instruct you in the ways of life—he/she may very well be a lowly but wise sheep herder "filled...with wisdom of heart" (many such are found in Scripture).

The fact that Bezaleel and Aholiab were **given** craftsmanship and teaching ability as two separate and distinct gifts from God, demonstrates that great talent doesn't automatically come with adequate ability to teach the skill to others.

Interestingly, most top level athletes hire coaches for themselves, demonstrating their belief that great skill doesn't often come with the additional gifts the teacher possesses. Conversely, most teachers of professionals don't have the "gift" of *exceptional* performance in the area they teach, yet they instruct the gifted professional—the truth is often perplexing, and causes many to stumble in their judgment.

$\approx$

Although not in the supernatural category this next story sheds light on our current conversation. At a early age Sean Foley became interested in the game of golf, not only from the perspective of a player but from that of a coach and teacher. However, it would take over twenty years for him to reach *ginōskō*, which has allowed him to, not just be a teacher of other men's methods but, transform his chosen profession.

This assessment is not an exaggeration. Remember, many of his professional coaching peers were vocal in their conviction that his methods and philosophy with Tiger's game were wrong and would fail. *The nerve of this unknown to think himself a member of the elite coaches in professional golf.* Few if any were vocal in their support for him (I can't recall a one.)

The main reason was because, historically, such dramatic change in playing philosophy and method resulted in failure. Another reason was, Foley's methods were "unorthodox", and appeared at first to be unsuccessful. In the face of criticism, and at the risk of a very short professional golf coaching career, he ignored the pressure to waver, and persisted toward success.

I believe a major part of Foley's success is due to **a genuine gift to teach**, evidenced by his uncanny ability to connect things which are at first glance unrelated to golf performance. Connecting geometry, physics, bio-mechanics, and human psychology to the game of golf is not new. However, to connect them all in a way that defies conventional logic, and does the "undoable", is remarkable.

Remember In chapter 4 my discussion on Why Most Savants and Prodigies Lack Experiential Knowledge, I said:

> *Knowing all the "facts" related to a subject is quite a bit different from knowing a thing inside-out, upside-down, and from many conceivable and inconceivable angles. The former is impressive, but the later makes it possible to connect your subject with everything it is minutely related to, because you see/understand more of its parts. When a related object or idea appears, the creatively gifted one is able to make the association with the subject, because she knows her subject intimately. She is then able to transform the world's appreciation by broadening their knowledge*

of the subject. This explains the difference between oida (knowledge/perception) and ginōskō (knowledge turned intimate).

Foley's gift allows him to recognize learning styles, and utilize different teaching and coaching methods to impart the same knowledge and skills to his professional clients and other students. Purportedly, Justin Rose, the successful professional golfer, is a thinker, and appreciates the precision of scientific theory; so Foley feeds him facts and theories necessary for improving his particular game. Hunter Mahan requires images and feelings, to which Foley coaches as if he were instructing Picasso to paint a canvas.

The inexplicable *gift* may indeed defy conventional logic.

Inability To Teach or To Learn?

There are times when failure can be attributed to the teacher's lack of skill or knowledge, and occasions when the failure rests with the student's inability to learn. The gifted teacher has the ability to overcome both of these, providing the student has the necessary prerequisite: a ***willingness to learn*** (after all we are talking about the highest intelligence on earth, so the *ability* to learn is generally assumed).

I am reminded of Mr. Jamie Escalante, whose gift of teaching was the subject of the movie *Stand and Deliver*. Mr. Escalante was a mathematics teacher at Garfield High School, a troubled inner-city school on the East side of Los Angeles. He taught teenagers who showed no interest in math—demonstrated by very low test scores—and taught them advanced mathematics including calculus.

I have to assume the teachers previously occupying his

position were *incapable* of or *unwilling* (I'm leaning toward the former) to teach those students the knowledge of mathematics they themselves possessed. At that time, it was popular for educators to believe inner-city children were incapable of comprehending any knowledge past the basics; therefore many teachers didn't even exert serious effort to pass on their knowledge.

In my opinion a *failure* to teach is a personal failure, arising from either apathy, or incompetence, or both—complete student failure belies the title "teacher." (If most of your students are failing you need another occupation.)

Escalante proved this by bringing the knowledge, and consequently the college placement test scores of those "high risk of failure" teenagers to so high a level it attracted the attention of the testing company, who expressed suspicions of student cheating. After retesting, the students again passed; they had indeed achieved the improbable, and mastered complex mathematics. His students went on to become scientists, engineers, and professors. The power of the gift to teach our own species, which is endowed with exceptional ability to learn, has extraordinary implications.

Many other examples of gifted teachers can be cited, but I'll just mention one more: Joe Clark, in New York City, played by Morgan Freeman in the movie about his teaching success, *Lean on Me*. Clark took his convictions to another level by demanding his teaching staff equip their children for exceptional performance in the real world they will face after graduation. We know he was effective because they made a movie out of his story. If the cognitive ability was encoded on the DNA, Clark was able to make it function up to its potential.

A "gift to teach" separates the great ones from the rest, as the teacher is able to intimately understand, not only with the head but the *heart*...not only the subject, but how it *should* be taught, and *can* be learned by the student.

In the case of Bezaleel and Aholiab, this gift was attributed to *Divine bestowment,* for the likes of Escalante and Clark, the gift, although not super natural (?), is nevertheless extraordinary and transcendent. Great teaching is always a gift.

God Given Ability to Learn

In the case of Bezaleel and Aholiab, the special ability to teach was a gift, but the ability to learn was also a gift to the students.[6] Apparently necessary because of the complexity of the task...the uniqueness of the items they were to produce (it would be like nothing in existence on planet earth)...and skill required for the tasks.

Why didn't God give everyone participating the gift he gave those two? How then would a leader (the correct one, or two) be determined—if any at all? Also, these exceptionally gifted individuals have *much broader* knowledge; their students would specialize in particular areas.

The instruction would develop the learning gift to full potential, so that the required skilled work force could be assembled. We have a record that the elaborate religious system of the Hebrew people was in fact constructed, and became a way of life for them for many years. Solomon's temple, a product of similar craftsmanship was an architectural marvel. There was also the Ark of the Covenant, one of the items produced by Bezaleel and Aholiab; many of us are familiar with it due

[6] This fact is implied in the passage quoted. pg. 236

to the popular *Raiders of the Lost Ark* movie based on this artifact.

Although this example of learning claims super-natural origin, we know that many geniuses and prodigies also have an innate, or suddenly acquired, gift for learning things at an extremely fast rate, which defies natural explanation.

There is such a thing as a special *gift* to learn.

Learning: Heredity or Gift

The ability of the brain to understand and learn things essential to our life on earth is without question. Programmed into the DNA of our species, and inherited from our ancestors, learning is a matter of existence and survival for the individual and the race. This is the reason the previously mentioned teacher believes *"almost everyone possesses the Heredity"* of something as essential to survival as music. However, music ability that transcends is on a whole different level, out of the reach of common learning; it accompanies learning ability in a student that usually surpasses their teacher's knowledge.

Foul Ball or Illegal Play?

Again, some are tempted to cry "foul or unfair" in response to the idea of **God given** talent and gifts. They reject any hint at the concept of **"the haves and have-nots,"** and they fear any suggestion of unfair treatment, and unequal allotment of gifts from a *fair* Creator: "surely a Creator would not discriminate when he distributes gifts would he?" Those who don't believe in God, believe fate operates without discrimination also; so gifts don't exist because **everyone has the same opportunities**.

Even if you ignore the fact that some people around are at a disadvantage when it comes to access to education and technology—how do we make sense of the obvious discrimination in the distribution of talent and ability among the rest of us

We must return to the laws of specialization and diversity. Simply put, the world appears to function on all levels through diversity of function and responsibility among the members within any organization or organism. **All members contribute to complete the whole organism, therefore "discrimination" in the sense of diversity and specialization is** *absolutely essential* **for any complex organism.**

Specialization also teaches us: all parts of the organism or organization are vitally important, and no one part can get too much credit.

Inexplicable gifts are a fact. The answer to the fear of unfair distribution of gifts then is wisdom and understanding of exactly how the world operates.

Next the answers to why this phenomenon and what it really means.

CHAPTER TWELVE

Let Us Have Dominion

*"...though He be not far from every one of us: For in Him
we live, and move, and have our being; as certain also of
your own poets have said, For we are also his offspring..."*
—*Acts*

Finally, how do we make sense of all that we've discovered
regarding The Zone Phenomenon? Allow me to remind
you how I began our expedition:

*"If we didn't have proof of its existence, we would
be tempted to think this idea of a "zone of super
human performance" to be the product of fantasy
and imagination...Think about the hurricane, tornado,
earthquake, all of these natural phenomena. What do
they say to us? They occur and make their mark in
a powerful and convincing way. We hurry to forget,
and hope they will not return, but we can't ignore their
power when they arise and disrupt our normality. They
are all forces to be reckoned with. So it is with the
incidents of The Zone Phenomena (TZP)...*

*Are we supposed to act like it doesn't mean anything?
We may attempt to ignore its influence, and forget
its brief appearances, but it too is undeniably a*

considerable force. It shakes our perception and reality...

Perhaps The Zone Phenomenon asserts its power and influence to tell us something about ourselves that we are unaware of or carelessly overlook. The tornado tells us how comparatively small and powerless we can be. But, maybe TZP tells us how powerful we could be...our true potential?"

It is on the last paragraph we will now concentrate our focus. Does this phenomenon in fact tell us how powerful we could be? There's no doubt the phenomenon of human life and consciousness is amazing in its normal state, but when we are empowered to lift 10 times our body weight...calculate complex equations at the speed of light...master the piano before we can spell music...remember everything we have ever read...know things we've never learned...then the meaning of the word phenomenal is stretched even further

WHAT IF PHENOMENAL WAS MEANT TO BE THE NORM?

In a video I created before finishing this book, I made this statement:

"Some genetic scientist would contribute these rare and extraordinary human feats to gene mutations, abnormalities...they are often classified as dysfunction. What if the opposite were true and they were meant to be the norm, and what we know as normal is actually the result of some kind of genetic mutation or abnormalities in the genes we inherited from our parents?"

Dr. Allan Snyder, an expert on Savant's, expected to un-cover autistic abnormalities when testing Rüdiger Gamm (pg. 59, 61) the math savant, but was surprised to discover his ex-traordinary gifts were not caused by a brain dysfunction.[1]

There is indeed another plausible explanation for the phe-nomenon of extraordinary human performance, other than freak occurrence or genetic mistake. To me, it's just as rea-sonable to conclude that genius potential lies below the sur-face, and was *accidentally*—better—*fortuitously* unleashed by a Zone incident.

Nevertheless, we are left with more questions to answer:

- Where exactly does this extraordinary ability come from—its ultimate source?

- What does it mean for us?

- Why is it uncommon and fleeting? And…

What Prevents Us from Living up to Our True Potential?

If the incredible people we've seen throughout this journey represent true human potential, most of us have and will die without living up to our true potential; why is this a fact? Why is "homeostasis" (normality, stability,) fixed below our true potential?

Our body has checks and balances built in, to assure we function in a normal, healthy—and hopefully optimal—way. If we drop below homeostasis, our body signals we are sick, and tries to correct us back to healthy/normal function. If we lag and need a boost, our body will call on "fight or flight

[1] http://un-conscious.com/videos/extraordinary-people-rudiger-gamm-part-1/

response" to increase our performance. If we don't wind back down to homeostasis, we will blow a fuse: have a nervous breakdown (nervous system overload): We need rest after overexertion. We've discussed previously how much demand is placed on the body's systems when we perform at maximum potential physically, and how unlikely it is to remain at that level. Our body therefore, keeps us somewhere between low and high performance.

Even permanent residents of The Zone like geniuses have only a narrow area of high performance, which is usually offset by areas of sub-par performance. Hence, homeostasis appears to be a **law**, in and outside of The Zone.

But, as we have seen, our *potential* is much higher. Why does it take extreme measures to reach higher performance? And why is it impossible to maintain if or when we get there? Back to these questions in a moment.

Dr. Traffert asks this question (left unanswered) in his introduction to *Islands of Genius*, pg. 12:

> *"How much does such actual knowledge, or at least the software templates or scaffolding for those rules of music, art and mathematics, or even other areas of expertise, come "factory installed" in all of us? That is an important, transcendental question."*

A quick attempt to answer this question, in light of what we have discovered so far in this book, would be to remind ourselves that the plans and power to create the brain in your skull, heart in your chest, and every other incredible part of us, is contained in written code inside of every cell. Cells are phenomena, invisible to your naked eye, and smaller than a single particle of dust. So, it is very easy to believe the rules for the principles of art or music—far less sophisticated then human life, could also be written in that code.

Spiritual Answers?

The facts and manifestations of this Zone type of transcendent human performance are real and impressive, begging an explanation for those of us who need to know "who we are," "what we are", "what is our true potential, and what force—if any—keeps us from living our potential?"

Because this is indeed a *"transcendental question,"* it is reasonable to describe it as a *spiritual question*; especially if it continues to defy any *natural, tangible* explanation. According to some experts, we've been around for millions of years (I'm inclined to disagree), nevertheless, we still can't answer these questions about ourselves satisfactorily.

WHO OR WHAT ARE WE

For an answer I turn to an ancient authority, written some 3,500 years ago (merely yesterday in evolutionary dating), at the beginning of recorded history on planet earth. The Book of Beginnings *Genesis,* written around 1416 B.C., by the man known in history as Moses, purports to chronicle the first 3,500 years (or so) of human history. Moses is credited with writing four books; copies of which are available today in hundreds, maybe thousands of languages. A very large number of people around the world embrace his writings. In fact, many people groups who don't rely on Moses' writings for early human history maintain similar versions of the same history, adding credibility to his accounts.

The history of the human race, recorded in the Book of Beginnings, answers this *transcendental question* by stating that "God" did in fact create man with these incredible gifts implanted within his body and being.

Some of you will say, "Now you have gone from tangible science, off into the world of religion, fantasy, and make believe...I was with you, but you're about to lose me."

Faith or Phenomena

I can understand your apprehension to venture into the realm of ideas and information which seem unscientific, and possibly require much *faith* to embrace.

I want to remind you, that up to this point we have been discussing the realm of *phenomenal* human performance, which itself would be a venture into fantasy, had it not been for the super powerful electron microscope which allowed us to see the hidden world of things like atoms and the genetic code. Who would have imagined that at our core is intelligent programming? The incidents of super human performance themselves would be comic book fantasy if we didn't witness them with our own eyes. **We are not venturing into the world of the super natural because we desire to go there— we are driven there. Or, like The Zone Phenomena: we have received an invitation.**

Scientists Agree

The first book I happened to purchase when I decided to write this book was *Brain States* by Tom Kenyon,[2] a scientist, psychotherapist, and musician,

---

[2] I credit "Brain States" for inspiring this books interior design model,

who pioneered methods of treating his patients with the aid of mood altering devices such as music. Dr. Kenyon, as a result of his research, knowledge, and experiences with the brain and its potential (I am speculating as to his motives), now claims to have been visited by aliens from outer space, who have a higher level of consciousness, and have shared their knowledge with him.[3] He in turn teaches others how to tap into the higher level of consciousness he believes to be innate within all of us. He is by no means alone among psychologists and neuroscientists with a super natural persuasion.

The scientific theory of evolution, that is the foundation of nearly every area of secular science, requires all who believe in it to believe in "theories" dating back billions of years, which can never be proven. Some scientists classify evolution itself as a religion because of the "faith" in hypothetical forces (like "chance", the Kuiper belt, and Oort cloud[4]) required to support its foundations.

My point is, that one cannot closely examine the incredible entity we are as human beings, especially our brains, and not be driven to reasoning and conclusions which transcend the bounds of our knowledge, and spill over into the metaphysical, super natural realm. This is a fact I have found with nearly all scientists who study the brain closely. This includes those who attempt to "keep their feet planted on earth" with the theory of evolution. Pick up any book on the natural and theoretical sciences or self actualization, and see for yourself if it doesn't convey some form of super natural ideas.

Is it reasonable to insist on a natural tangible explanation for something intangible and absolutely transcendent?

[3] http://tomkenyon.com/who-are-the-hathors
[4] http://astroengine.com/2008/08/22/why-cant-we-see-the-oort-cloud/

Make no mistake about it: the DNA code may be a tangible chemical language, but communication, and meaning (from idea, to language, to conscious reality) is intangible, immaterial, and spiritual. Where does the *intent, will, desire,* that sets DNA dialog in motion, come from? All intelligent communication is intentional. Add the element of nearly incomprehensible human performance, and *intangible* answers must be pursued.

If you have a hard time considering the Divinely inspired Moses' record, how will you believe when I tell you of the 23 year old, 120 pound woman who lifted a 1500 pound car...or that a grown man became a math genius and gifted artist after a brutal mugging?

I hope I've convinced you to stay with me until the end.

How Exactly Does Moses State These Details?

In his creation narrative, Moses records the Creator as assessing his work, *"And God saw everything that He had made and behold, it was very good."*[5]

Now, first of all, we may second guess Moses' authority to claim inspiration for his statements (he speaks for God) as to the origin of men and our world. But we have to admit, he has as much a right as any other historian or scientist to offer a reasonable explanation for the pressing question, "Who are we?" We have already seen people who instantly knew things they have never learned, why couldn't Moses have had the truth about the origin of the human race revealed to him likewise?

Not without weight, is the accuracy of his historical writ-

---

[5] Genesis 1:31

ings on events *before, during,* and *after* his own lifetime—he wrote many accurate prophecies of future events. That said, any view has the right to be examined, embraced, or rejected based on the weight of the argument, credibility of evidence, or if the information is impossible to disprove by absolute contradictory facts, it must be considered by reasonable men.

In the absence of absolute, irrefutable facts disproving Moses' statements in his book *Genesis,* let's continue our look at what he had to say about who we are and our potential.

Usefulness and Purpose

Moses records the creator (Elohim) as acknowledging his entire creation was *"very good."* Now, we can take a look outside and agree, yes this is a very good thing. Our world is marvelously put together and ordered. The sun, sky, wind, plant-life, birds of the air, the oceans, the life in them, and us, are "oh so very good".

Now, if the tree, for example, was said to be "pleasant to see, and good for food,"[6] (two of its intended purposes), then *"good"* must include the ideas of **usefulness and purpose. A tree that should bear fruit, but doesn't would not be "very good."**

All other forms of life are impressively adapted to their specific environments (domains). The birds masterfully navigate the air, build their nests, navigate the seasons, and everything necessary to their existence. Trees and plants faithfully do their part for our delicate ecosystem.

Just the other day I saw several vultures. They looked like eagles from a distance, with broad wingspans, soaring grace-

---

[6] Genesis 2:9

fully in 30 mile per hour winds on a chilly day. If I were their manufacturer, I would say I did a very good job. The same can be said for the myriads of fascinating insects, land animals, plant, and sea life. If "very good" means they are more than adequately suited to function up to their intended purpose, ability, and potential, then it is an appropriate description, because they do so in a marvelous and beautiful way.

What About Us?

Now, as for man, what is his potential? The man and woman were "very good" for their intended purpose, which is declared to be, **"rule/subdue/have dominion"** (as the supreme creation, made in the very image or likeness of God), over everything created on earth. The whole earth was their intended domain:

> *"And God said, Let us make man in our image, after our likeness: and let them have dominion over the fish of the sea, and over the fowl of the air, and over the cattle, and over all the earth, and over every creeping thing that creeps upon the earth. So God created man in his own image, in the image of God created he him; male and female created he them." —Genesis 1*

If God had indeed accomplished His purpose in creating man "in His image and likeness," then man was certainly endowed with incredible ability; phenomenal, extraordinary, transcendent ability is more like it—to say the least.

What would constitute "very good" as a description of living out this intended purpose? "Very good" would have to include the potential and ability to perceive, understand, and accomplish the things—not only possible in this world—but essential, like music, art, mathematics, harmony, beauty, symmetry, science, etc; *"let them have dominion over all..."*

It would be impossible for man to rule the earth without this knowledge, given to him by his Creator as a part of the "package," installed on the hard drive, just like lower animals and plants. This knowledge is original equipment. **Anything less would not be a "very good" thing, because man would be ill-equipped for his intended purpose.** Especially if the lesser creatures are exceptionally well equipped with "instincts" to rule their domains. Should the songbird be better equipped for music than man? This is suggested in the text, as God brings all of the animals to Adam for naming: A monumental task from our perspective—apparently no problem for Adam.

For the Creator to leave man without the knowledge and skills required to rule over all the earth, would be like creating the sun for light and heat but leaving out the radiant energy.

Assuming Moses was truly inspired to write his explanation for the existence of the world as we know it, and man in particular, we have a very good explanation for the incredible feats savants, geniuses, and Zone residents are able to accomplish: **We are fashioned in the Creator's likeness, and endowed with superior knowledge and abilities above anything on earth; it's installed on our hard drive, written in our DNA.**

WHY MEDIOCRITY IS THE NORM

However, the question still remains as to why we don't or can't perform up to the greater potential demonstrated in TZP by athletes, artists, musicians, geniuses, savants, and those forced into incredible exploits by unusual circumstances? Why are these feats rare? If greatness is on the hard drive, why is homeostasis set so low?

Well, Moses had an answer for that question also, which he records in the same book: Genesis. **Moses' answer explains the theories and conclusions suggested by scientists, researchers, and curious observers: There was something that obstructed, damaged, or impaired, that "very good" manufactured product we know as man.**

Scientists spend millions trying to identify *genes, viruses, bacteria, etc.,* which cause certain ailments. In other words, seeking to identify and *remove barriers* to optimal health and performance. Scientists have, for ages, looked for a "fountain of youth," a key to *unlock* longevity, because death itself is a mystery that is hard—if not impossible—to explain by scientific reason. We should *theoretically* live longer. At least we shouldn't deteriorate so rapidly, and should easily live a few hundred years (that's my conservative guess). Best scientific estimations, based on the average health of humans *today* is that, 120 years should be our potential life span. But if many plants and animals live much longer than that, we should possess more life then they...shouldn't we?

∾

In the meantime there is the idea of **"meaning." Am I nothing?** Is my self-consciousness, my identity, my unique person, meaningless concepts? Shouldn't I be an everlasting entity? Are 80 years of earthly existence (most of which is immature youth, and old age) all there is to me? Again, there are trees that have lived my life span over—10 times. Who is actually "ruling the earth?"

In 2004, Robert Mitchell, professor of biology at Penn State, discusses this puzzle from a biological perspective:

> *"It was always thought that once you took human cells out of the body and grew them in a dish they would divide and divide and divide and not age. In the sixties, we learned that there is a limit to how many times a cell could divide in a dish. They do age and have a limited lifespan. We know now there is some kind of a clock that limits the longevity of these cells. That discovery in the sixties led hundreds of investigators to start working with human cells in culture—we say in vitro—to see what it was that was limiting their life span. That's called the Hayflick limit, the limited number of times a cell is able to divide."*[7]

Professor Mitchell was talking about *death*, the limited lifespan of human cells.

Moses recorded the event which damaged man's ability to function the way he was ***originally intended*** by his creator. I **like to interpret that event as a malfunction, a functional breakdown, a thing built to be "very good" performing "very bad."**

Conditional Privilege

As Moses tells the story, the first humans were manufactured according to the "likeness of God," "in His image," so as to rule over all other earthly things. Apparently that position of "God likeness" was ***conditional***, a ***privilege***, that is, it was dependant on the man and woman maintaining a proper relationship with the One whose person they were a reflection of. You might think of that *malfunction* as a high treason, aligning with the enemy, type of thing.

---

[7] http://www.rps.psu.edu/time/humans.html

Moses puts it this way:

*"And the LORD God commanded the man, saying, Of every tree of the garden you may freely eat: But of the tree of the knowledge of good and evil, you shall not eat of it: for in the day that you eat thereof you shall surely **die**...And He said to the man, Because you have listened to the voice of your wife, and have eaten of the tree about which I commanded you, saying, You shall not eat from it, the ground shall be cursed because of you; you shall eat of it in sorrow all the days of your life. And it shall bring forth thorns and thistles for you, and you shall eat the plant of the field. By the sweat of your face you shall eat bread until your return to the ground. For you have been taken out of it; for you are dust, and to dust you shall return."*
-Genesis 2,3

It is implied that man lost his *privileged* "very good" position in the world. That which was intended to be easy, would now require labor, and considerable effort. I am assuming his mental and physical performance was affected by that *sentence of death*.

Some scholars may object to the narrative at this point, suggesting it resembles too closely a fairy tale with such a ***petty test*** from a supremely intelligent being (Deity). Where are the more noble ideas of forgiveness and love, after so small an infraction? I would answer: the test of loyalty and privilege is best to be a small thing rather than a big thing; If you can't trust a friend in a small thing, you have exposed a *very serious* personal flaw. This *small* misstep is akin to a well fed, spoiled, filthy rich, son, stealing a dollar from his dad's wallet.

What do you do with a product that no longer functions as you manufactured it to function?

It appears from the narrative that the superior endowments of the man and woman above all other created things, was a *privilege*, subject to their worthiness for such a position so close to their Creator (God). It is said in the narrative that Adam and Eve (the first man and woman) talked with God in the garden: suggesting the type of relationship and communication which included ability, on man's part, to comprehend, at least some of what his creator would be sharing with them. God also brought all the animals to Adam to see what he would name them. **Adam and Eve's level of intelligence had to be on the level of an unrestricted, unencumbered Savants, without the restrictions of specialized, narrow knowledge, and limited brain resources.**

Death Transmitted

The **condition** for maintaining the privilege granted to Adam and Eve as bearer of their Creator's "image" was *obedience*."The *genetic defect* (cellular death,[8]) incurred by Adam—a son of God—and Eve his wife, is transmitted to all of their offspring (heredity). The most obvious proof in favor of this assertion is physical deterioration and death within the species.

This also explains why normal performance, homeostasis, is held above poor, but well below the maximum potential we glimpse in TZP—we inherit the sentence of death at our genetic core. Death is transmitted along with life.

THE STORY DOESN'T END HERE

Because we may hope for a positive ending to this journey to "unlock the secrets of The Zone Phenomenon," I will attempt to provide just that in this last and final section. After all, we

[8] As Professor Mitchell referenced, see pg 256

have identified the roads to The Zone, its potential residents, how it operates, including its power source, roadblocks, and obstacles which would prevent entry, a number of keys which open the gate into this region, the laws which govern this state, and the likely reason for the existence of this phenomenal territory in the first place.

Are we now, based on Genesis, left with the conclusion that all of us are **permanently hindered** from reaching that level of performance and staying there?

You've likely picked this book up because you are interested in obtaining maximum performance for yourself or someone you care about. I hope you have found information and advice that will help you in that pursuit. However, the reality is: no matter what level of performance you reach in this life it will not last, it is only fleeting, as old age and death imminently awaits us all.[9]

I truly hate to be the bearer of bad news. I understand I am taking a risk turning you off, with what may at first appear to be a sour note, but actually it's not.

This entire book is about observing the facts, extracting meaning, and making some application to our lives. I would therefore be remiss to overlook or neglect to make some attempt to close the gaping hole in our hopes imposed by the powerful realities of age deterioration and death.

The Hope: The Second Adam

Moses introduced us to the cause of mankind's plight, which originated with Adam and Eve, the source of our defective

---

[9] Unless you follow Jack LaLanne (A Zone resident) who-at the age of 70-towed 70 people in 70 row boats while swimming one mile. http://goo.gl/4vfMT

genes. But, the story doesn't end there. The same Bible which contains The Book of Beginnings also contains the record of the man it calls "the second Adam."

(As I mentioned earlier: I truly have an aversion to fantasy, except for entertainment purposes, so this book deals with serious non-fiction matters. I have labored to share only the facts.)

The rest of the Old Testament of the Bible, after Adam and Eve's fall from privilege, is devoted to chronicling *how* God set about to accomplish the restoration of the privileged—and may I add—phenomenal relationship mankind once enjoyed:

"And I will put enmity between you (the serpent) and the woman, and between your seed and her Seed; He will bruise your head, and you shall bruise His heel." [10]

The New Testament of the bible is devoted to the historical record of God fulfilling this very promise he made to Adam and Eve after their disobedience and subsequent punishment. The "seed" of the woman (one of her offspring), would sever the "ties to evil"—so to speak—and would, according to other scripture, be referred to as "the second Adam:"[11]

*"But now Christ has been raised from the dead; He became the first fruit of those having fallen asleep. For since death is through man, also through a Man is a resurrection of the dead; for as in Adam all die, so also in Christ all will be made alive...So also it has been written, "The" first "man", Adam, "became a living soul;" **the last Adam** a life-giving Spirit...The first man was out of earth, earthy. The second Man was the Lord out of Heaven...Such as is the earthy man, such also are the earthy ones. And such as is the*

[10] Gen 3:15
[11] 1Cor. 15, Romans 5

heavenly Man, such also are the heavenly ones. And as we bore the image of the earthy man, we shall also bear the image of the heavenly Man.

To simplify these passages in plain English: the first Adam caused death for his offspring; the second Adam gives life to his posterity. These statements from scripture promise a full restoration of all that the first Adam lost, and that is accomplished through the second Adam. As all men have borne the earthly image of the first Adam, so, some will bear the non-earthly image of the second Adam (Christ).

The guarantee of the second Adam's ability to transmit this *life to those who are otherwise dying,* is the fact that he resurrected himself from the dead. He experienced a complete reversal of deterioration, accompanying earthly limitations, and death.

The *secrets* of unlocking this super natural phenomenon are disclosed within the New Testament of the Bible, which reveal Jesus Christ, the second Adam.

Phenomenon or Fiction

Once again we are presented with a phenomenon, which may appear to be the product of fantasy and imagination. Remember, we believe a particle smaller than a speck of dust, with a computer program in its center, triggers itself to transform into a human being. If we believe that, how much greater a leap is it to believe in a resurrection. Fortunately for us who require more tangible evidence to support such claims of a super human feat such as *life after death*, we have a plethora of historical records of the birth, life, death, and resurrection of Jesus Christ—the Second Adam. Although these historical records stretch our minds, and tear our ties to normality; like TZP itself, I have no compelling reason to dismiss them.[12] *Are we supposed to act like it doesn't mean anything?*

On the contrary; the greatest factor convincing me the Bible record is trustworthy, is the large number of prophecies, predicting events hundreds of years before they actually occurred: There are at least **2,000 such prophecies** written at different times in history by a large number of men (39).[13]

So then, for us who are convinced by the scriptures, there is yet an opportunity—moreover, a promise—to realize our full phenomenal potential; A hope of unhindered, unending, UNCONSCIOUS, extraordinary human performance.

In the meantime: knowledge, and I hope books like this, can help us minimize mediocrity, and maximize our *existing* potential for experiencing The Zone Phenomenon on planet earth.

> *You made him a little less than the angels; You crowned him with glory and honor; and "You set him over the works of Your hands. You subjected all things under his feet."... But now we do not yet see all things being subject to him...—Heb. 2:7,8*

The End

Thanks for letting me be your guide into the Zone region. Enjoy your stay or have a safe trip home.

---

[12] If you are interested in examining some of these records there are many books which tackle the subject such as Josh McDowell's,, *Evidence That Demands a Verdict.*

[13] http://www.reasons.org/articles/articles/fulfilled-prophecy-evidence-for-the-reliability-of-the-bible

[ACKNOWLEDGMENTS]

After all this discussion on extraordinary human potential and performance, I must thank the one who makes our participation in this marvelous phenomenon (life itself) possible. (Not to mention the future hope we discussed in the last chapter.) In the words of the apostle, describing the Lord Jesus: *"Now, to the King eternal, incorruptible, invisible, the only wise God, be honor and glory forever and ever. Amen."*

Although I have written and shared my own thoughts in the past, this—my first full-book project—has been a grind at times. Verbally arguing my opinions is very different from creating a record of them for all to critique—forever. The pressures of research, clear and effective communication, and creativity—to name a few—added to the pressure.

At those times I am grateful to have had family and friends to lean on for support. My sister Judy, who's enthusiasm for this book project over the past few years, was a frequent and reliable source for me to stop and re-fill my gas tank. Thanks for taking my calls, and insisting I finish this race. My daughter Valerie, who not only encouraged Dad, but proof-read, and grammar checked the manuscript along the way: thanks sweetie, Dad loves you:-) Rosita, Anthony, Vonda, Angela my siblings: thanks for supporting me; especially when I needed an early kickstart.

My longtime friend, and fellow soldier in Christ, Richard Leggett, who provided meaningful support to me as I shaped the outline and arguments for several sections of this book, as well as gave time to help with the final proof-reading. Thanks friend!

John Ball, I could not have started this project with sta-

264 | UNCONSCIOUS: Secrets of The Zone...

ble footing without your enthusiastic help. Kim Clifton, your words of encouragement after reading the first draft were a frequent motivation for me to reflect upon over the past two years.

I am truly thankful for all of my friends who positively encouraged and supported me. To everyone who will read this book, thanks for considering this book worth your time; I hope it exceeded your expectations.

Last but not least, all of my teachers, who's scholarly books, blogs, articles, and videos I relied upon to complete this project: thanks for sharing your knowledge with the world.

I am a fortunate guy because of you all!

Contact Information:

jwwalkjr@gmail.com

EUTHUS PUBLISHING
5300 N. Braeswood Blvd. Ste. 4-151
Houston, TX 77096

Made in the USA
Columbia, SC
04 February 2023

11731776R00164